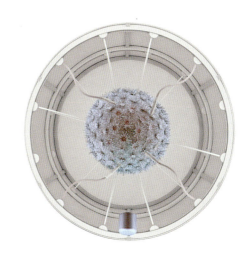

Guest-edited by
Mark Garcia

POSTHUMAN ARCHITECTURES

THEORIES, DESIGNS, TECHNOLOGIES AND FUTURES

01 | Vol 94 | 2024

POSTHUMAN ARCHITECTURES:
THEORIES, DESIGN, TECHNOLOGIES AND FUTURES

01/2024

About the Guest-Editor — 5 Mark Garcia	**On the Posthuman Charm of Slime and Mould** — 46 Mario Carpo
Introduction — 6 **The Posthuman in Architectures and Other Spaces** Mark Garcia	**Alternative Domiciles for the Domestic Posthuman** — 52 Colbey Reid and Dennis Weiss
More-Than-Post — 14 A Five-Step Recipe for Decentring Design Jacopo Leveratto	**Aliens Among Us** — 62 The Posthuman *Wunderkammer* Andrew Witt
A Posthuman Architectural Artificial Intelligence *Speculum*? — 22 Text and Images in Future Spaces Alberto Fernández González and Mark Garcia	
Disruptive Ecologies — 30 Design with Nonhuman Intelligences Roberto Bottazzi, Tyson Hosmer and Mollie Claypool	
Feral Surfaces — 38 Building Envelopes as Intelligent Multi-species Habitats Ariane Lourie Harrison	

52

ISSN 0003-8504   ISBN 978 1 394 17003 6   Guest-edited by **Mark Garcia**

Alternate Architectural Subjects   70

An Apple Tree That Lived on Long Island

Sylvia Lavin

Beyond Domesticities   76

Posthuman Architectures for Animals We Farm

Paul Dobraszczyk

Flying Feral   84

Posthuman Architectures, Enclosures and Open-Loop Interface Designs

Steven Hutt

Learning, Teaching, Coexisting, Thriving   94

The Evolution of Space Architecture in the Posthuman Era

Olga Bannova and Sandra Häuplik-Meusburger

Scaling Lunar Habitats from Research Outposts to Thriving Villages   100

Xavier De Kestelier, Levent Ozruh and Jonathan Irawan

Posthuman Space Architecture   110

Machine Worlds to Seed Space

Brent Sherwood

21st-Century Posthuman Spaceship and Spacecraft Architectures   118

Mark Garcia

> 'Ultimately posthuman architecture points to the idea that in some cases the not-just-human, the no-architect and no-architecture constitutes the ideal or optimal design act'
> — Mark Garcia

From Another Perspective

The Ultimate Sin   128

The Super-Surrealist Body

Neil Spiller

Contributors   134

Editorial Offices
John Wiley & Sons
9600 Garsington Road
Oxford
OX4 2DQ

T +44 (0)18 6577 6868

Editor
Neil Spiller

Managing Editor
Caroline Ellerby
Caroline Ellerby Publishing

Freelance Contributing Editor
Abigail Grater

Publisher
Todd Green

Art Direction + Design
Christian Küsters
Mihaela Mincheva
CHK Design

Production Editor
Elizabeth Gongde

Prepress
Artmedia, London

Printed in the United Kingdom
by Hobbs the Printers Ltd

Front cover
Jason Hopkins,
Abstract Figure: Achilles, 2022.
© Jason Hopkins /
abhominal.com/t:
@_abhominal_art

Inside front cover
Bricolo Falsarella, Lugana
Winery, Lugana, Italy, 2023.
© Filippo Bricolo

Page 1
Certain Measures,
The Observatory,
Museum of the Future, Dubai,
United Arab Emirates, 2022.
Image courtesy Certain
Measures

EDITORIAL BOARD

Denise Bratton
Paul Brislin
Mark Burry
Helen Castle
Nigel Coates
Peter Cook
Kate Goodwin
Edwin Heathcote
Brian McGrath
Jayne Merkel
Peter Murray
Mark Robbins
Deborah Saunt
Patrik Schumacher
Jill Stoner
Ken Yeang

ARCHITECTURAL DESIGN

January/February **2024** Volume **94** Issue **01**

Disclaimer
The Publisher and Editors cannot be held responsible for errors or any consequences arising from the use of information contained in this journal; the views and opinions expressed do not necessarily reflect those of the Publisher and Editors, neither does the publication of advertisements constitute any endorsement by the Publisher and Editors of the products advertised.

Journal Customer Services
For ordering information, claims and any enquiry concerning your journal subscription please go to www.wileycustomerhelp.com/ask or contact your nearest office.

Americas
E: cs-journals@wiley.com
T: +1 877 762 2974

Europe, Middle East and Africa
E: cs-journals@wiley.com
T: +44 (0)1865 778 315

Asia Pacific
E: cs-journals@wiley.com
T: +65 6511 8000

Japan (for Japanese-speaking support)
E: cs-japan@wiley.com
T: +65 6511 8010

Visit our Online Customer Help available in 7 languages at www.wileycustomerhelp.com/ask

Print ISSN: 0003-8504
Online ISSN: 1554-2769

All prices are subject to change without notice.

Identification Statement
Periodicals Postage paid at Rahway, NJ 07065. Air freight and mailing in the USA by Mercury Media Processing, 1850 Elizabeth Avenue, Suite C, Rahway, NJ 07065, USA.

USA Postmaster
Please send address changes to *Architectural Design*, John Wiley & Sons Inc., c/o The Sheridan Press, PO Box 465, Hanover, PA 17331, USA

Rights and Permissions
Requests to the Publisher should be addressed to:
Permissions Department
John Wiley & Sons Ltd
The Atrium
Southern Gate
Chichester
West Sussex PO19 8SQ
UK

F: +44 (0)1243 770 620
E: Permissions@wiley.com

All Rights Reserved. No part of this publication may be reproduced, stored in a retrieval system or transmitted in any form or by any means, electronic, mechanical, photocopying, recording, scanning or otherwise, except under the terms of the Copyright, Designs and Patents Act 1988 or under the terms of a licence issued by the Copyright Licensing Agency Ltd, 5th Floor, Shackleton House, Battle Bridge Lane, London SE1 2HX, without the permission in writing of the Publisher.

△ is published bimonthly and is available to purchase as individual volumes at the following prices.

Individual copies:
£29.99 / US$45.00
Mailing fees for print may apply

ABOUT THE
GUEST-EDITOR

MARK GARCIA

Mark Garcia is a London-based academic, author, journalist and photographer. His PhD 'The 21st-Century Posthuman Architectural Design of Spacecraft and Spaceships, is supervised by Professor Mario Carpo and Professor Nat Chard, as part of the Architecture and Digital Theory (ADT) research programme directed by Professor Frédéric Migayrou and Professor Mario Carpo at the Bartlett School of Architecture, University College London (UCL). He holds a BA degree in the History of Art and Philosophy from UCL, and an MSc in International Business from Birkbeck College, University of London. As a lecturer at the Bartlett, he teaches on the B-Pro Architectural Design MA (History and Theory) and is the coordinator of the Master of Research (MRes) and Architecture and Digital Theory PhD Programme Seminar. From 2020 to 2022 he designed and led the school's '21st Century London Architectures' BA module in the Department of History of Art. He was previously a Senior Lecturer at the University of Greenwich, London, where he redesigned and led the two 'Histories/Theories/Futures' MArch thesis modules. Prior to this he was Research Co-ordinator at the Royal College of Art's School of Innovation Design Engineering, and Deputy Head and Head of Research in the Department of Architecture and Interiors. From 1997 to 2001 he worked as an academic researcher and project manager at St Antony's College, University of Oxford, under Professor Sir Theodore Zeldin.

Mark has also worked in practice, at Branson Coates Architecture and at Skidmore, Owings & Merrill (SOM) in London, in research, development and marketing. He has published articles in *Building Design* and the *Architectural Review*, and has been a regular contributor to △. He is the Guest-Editor of the △ issues *Architextiles* (November/December 2006), *Patterns of Architecture* (November/December 2009), and *Future Details of Architecture* (July/August 2014), and the editor of *The Diagrams of Architecture* (John Wiley & Sons, 2010). He has lectured at universities in Japan, Canada, Germany, the US, Switzerland and the Republic of Ireland. He was the inaugurating guest panellist for the opening symposium of the 2017 Southern California Institute of Architecture (SCI-Arc) exhibition 'Close Up', and the keynote lecturer for the 2019 'Experimental Diagramming' exhibition at the Berlin Architekturmuseum and Technical University of Berlin. His 2017 'Up Close' solo show of photographs of the models of Zaha Hadid was exhibited at Cornell University College of Architecture, Art, and Planning. His 114-minute film *REDroom REDux* about David Lynch's spatial design of his *Twin Peaks* 25-year film and TV project was screened at the University of Greenwich and featured as part of the Hawksmoor International Lecture Series in 2018. △

Text © 2024 John Wiley & Sons Ltd. Image © Mark Garcia

THE POSTHUMAN IN ARCHITECTURES AND OTHER SPACES

INTRODUCTION

MARK GARCIA

Posthuman Architecture [...] There has not been an architecture of similar vigour in 100 years [...]
A new architecture is born beyond our attention [...]
There is no tradition [...] There is no context [...]
There is nothing.

— Rem Koolhaas, *Countryside: A Report*, 2020[1]

Though the term 'posthuman' was coined in 1977 by the Egyptian scholar Ihab Hassan,[2] for some scholars[3] the posthuman *avant la lettre* has always (back to ancient Egypt) coexisted with the human. For others[4] we became posthuman in the 20th century.

Posthumanisms are responses to human bodies developing in new ways, human minds and brains being altered in recent neurological, epistemological ways which effect equally young forms of evolution (ie auto-evolution), reproduction, the agent (ie as holobiont – symbiotic

Empty stainless-steel cleanroom prepared for installation

The Modernist cleanroom was invented in the US in 1960. Cleanrooms are always getting 'cleaner'. An ISO 14644-1 level 1-certified cleanroom is the cleanest ever, for now. Designed for and inhabited mostly or only by robots and machines (to make microchips, batteries or spacecraft; to handle radioactive materials, nanotech or living pathogens; or in medical/life-sciences and exobiological laboratories/operating theatres), they are one of the most posthuman, hyper-rationalised and controlled interiors of the regime of ultra-techno-minimalism, unknown to previous versions of Modernism.

host-based micro ecosystem) and of identity and the subject's phenomenological sensorium. They are responses to relatively novel planetary-scale contexts and conditions where technologies and other nonhuman assemblages and entities are having such profound impacts that these are now confounding human understanding and therefore out of our control. Some of these drivers depend on contested definitions of 'life', 'vital' and 'animate', 'sentient' and 'conscious' – particularly in reference to biological organisms and now artificial intelligence (AI), but also partly because experts disagree on definitions of 'human', 'life' and 'self'. Posthumanists now refer to the 'post-person'.[5] The consequences of this alternative, networked, systemic, extended and augmented 'I' is multiply located and dynamic. It acknowledges more malleable affiliations and aspirations rather than simplistic, permanent and received identities.

Daniela Yaneva,
Down House in AD 2099,
2019

above: Part of a posthuman project based on a speculative futurology for Down House, Charles Darwin's home in Kent, England, which he owned and occupied from 1842. In this posthuman permutation, the re-natured house becomes sentient and begins to redesign itself, finally escaping into the surrounding landscape to redesign that. The ultimate return of a posthumanly evolved but architecturalised biology to the countryside.

Throughout the 21st century, 'posthuman' began involuting and conspicuously complicating to include (amongst others) the transhuman, nonhuman, humanity 2.0, after-human, neocybernetic, subhuman, a-human, blue-posthuman, neo-human, infra-human, alter-human, ultra-human, other-than-human, beyond-human – almost any prefix-human. The most well-known of these in relation to but often contrasted with posthumanisms are the more controversial and more politically fractious 'transhumanisms' and the more radically left-leaning metahumanisms. Notably, the posthuman includes the xeno/alien and even the absurd 'post-posthuman'.

Tamar Sharon's *Human Nature in an Age of Biotechnology* (2014)[6] provides perhaps the most rigorous and robust taxonomy of posthumanisms by distinguishing them on three continuous scales of 'optimist–pessimist' (including liberal, radical and dystopic posthumanisms), 'historical/materialist–philosophical/ontological' (including 'anti-humanisms' and 'methodological posthumanism') and 'humanist–non-humanist' axes. Other major divisions do however exist, such as those between bio- and techno-posthumanisms and divisions in relation to disciplines, practices, professions and geography.

Mario Carpo and Mark Garcia with Steven Hutt,
Digital Architectures Chronogram,
From the Chronograms of Architecture
(e-flux Architecture and the Jencks Foundation),
2023

opposite top: The historiographic context, concepts and contents of posthuman architectures in relation to the histories, technologies, designs and theories of architecture from 1940 to the present. Based on a hand-drawn diagram and essay by Mario Carpo for eflux: https://www.e-flux.com/architecture/chronograms/.

Alberto Fernández González and Mark Garcia,
Phase II Synthesis 851847497740d298991,
Posthuman AIchitectural Speculations,
2023

right: The result of a number of autophagous image-based and textual prompts for the terms 'posthuman architecture', this is the result generated by the artificial intelligence (AI). Apparently a hybrid of greenhouses, Google/Amazon-style mega-corporate campuses and planetary-based space architecture, landscape architecture and advanced digital design, this urban-scaled series of transparent/translucent dome-shell architectures is in an unspecified location and for an unspecified ecosystem of unknown inhabitant subjects.

Alberto Fernández González and Mark Garcia,
Phase II Synthesis no 6266214885470011558,
Posthuman AIchitectural Speculations,
2023

opposite bottom: An AI response to the words 'posthuman interiors' captures a synthesis of what appears to be multi-storey botanical, hydroponic or agricultural farming with a data centre, factory, laboratory, fulfilment centre, storage depot and perhaps even a corporate campus, transport or delivery interchange – all under a contemporary non-standard, digitally designed and manufactured glass or ethylene tetrafluoroethylene (ETFE) roof?

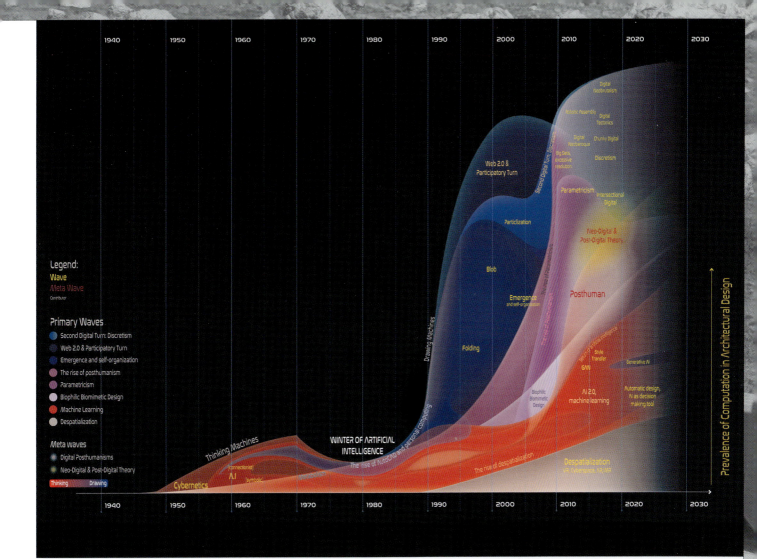

From a survey of the recent media (which includes speculative and fictional content from films, art, literature, television and 'new' and 'social' media), the three most salient and general groupings of indicators, qualities, elements and drivers of posthumanness (depending on the type of these that determines the architecture) are those prioritising or wholly consisting of, firstly, the biological/genetic; secondly, those privileging the abiotic digital-mechanical; and thirdly and most inclusively, a nonbinary nature-culture hybrid of the two former categories. This more expanded third 'posthuman' treats 'nature-culture' as a singular entangled term. The 'new' media of the third type in particular form the *de facto*, if not the *de novo* media of the most complex posthuman architectures being generated in the present. The result is that posthumanisms can be as mutually antithetical, polysemous, contested and contingent as Modernisms and Postmodernisms became.

Posthumanologies and Posthumanising Spaces

Leaving aside for now that some nonhumans display culture, technology and the ability to build, the first posthuman architectures were not only tents and huts but also found or augmented caves, hollow trees, arboreal platforms/nests or sheltered pits and tunnels. If we are already posthuman and live in an arguably posthuman world, then all architecture is (weakly) posthuman. In a stronger sense, posthuman architecture is architecture for or by posthuman subjects – humans, nonhumans or mixes of these. Posthuman architecture is also architecture that uses posthumans, is in posthuman locations or conditions, is for posthuman purposes, typologies and programmes or has posthuman elements. Posthumanisation is also a process – an architecture or space with a posthumanising affect or effect. In the context of the Third Machine Age and the Fourth Industrial Revolution, posthuman spaces and architectures are driving an architectural revaluation of values whereby posthuman architecture is the consequence of extending equality, diversity and inclusion (EDI) to all subjects and agencies. Posthuman EDI is *the* EDI. It is *the* spatial justice, as it includes zones beyond Earth.

Historical and theoretical publications on posthuman architecture go as far back as K Michael Hays's *Modernism and the Posthumanist Subject* (1992)[7] but were still very few even after 2010. Less explicitly posthuman, Mark Wigley and Beatriz Colomina used 'Super-Humanity'[8] for the title of their Istanbul Design Biennial in 2020, whilst Liam Young in his *D Machine Landscapes* (2019) issue prefers 'Post-Anthropocene',[9] and for Andrés Jaque it is 'More-than-Human'.[10]

Some of the most posthuman examples of these include the International Thermonuclear Experimental Reactor (ITER) in southeastern France; the National Satellite Test Facility in Oxfordshire, UK; the US's Laser Interferometer Gravitational-Wave Observatory (LIGO) facilities in Hanford, Washington and Livingston, Louisiana; plus spaceports, recycling centres, augmented- and mixed-reality architectures, telescopes and observatories, neutrino detectors, zoos and aquariums, garages, datacentres, mission control centres, cleanrooms, the metaverse, botanical architectures, transport interchanges, cryogenic vacuum chambers, super-sewers, underwater sculpture parks, super-offices, oceanographic research stations, the Orfield Lab Anechoic chamber in Minneapolis (the quietest place on Earth), the 'Deep Dive' pool in Dubai (the world's deepest artificial pool), super-factories, quantum supercomputer labs, Apple's 'Smart Home', long-stay vehicles (eg submarines and cruise ships), automated/robotic farms, storage and preservation spaces, research and development (R&D) labs, wildlife reserves, airports, the internet and space architectures. But not all posthuman spaces (such as the Naica Crystal Caves in Mexico) are posthuman architectures.

The Red Room from *Twin Peaks*, Series 3, Episode 1, 2018

below: Twin Peaks is a posthuman total-artwork spanning over 25 years, seven music albums, three series over 48 episodes, 5 major books and a major cinema feature film. The Red Room has an interior but no exterior. One of the greatest and most famous rooms ever designed, it is the mission control for the town of Twin Peaks (designed by director David Lynch and Mark Frost from 1990 to 2018) and has its own but unknown agencies and forces that extend across the planet.

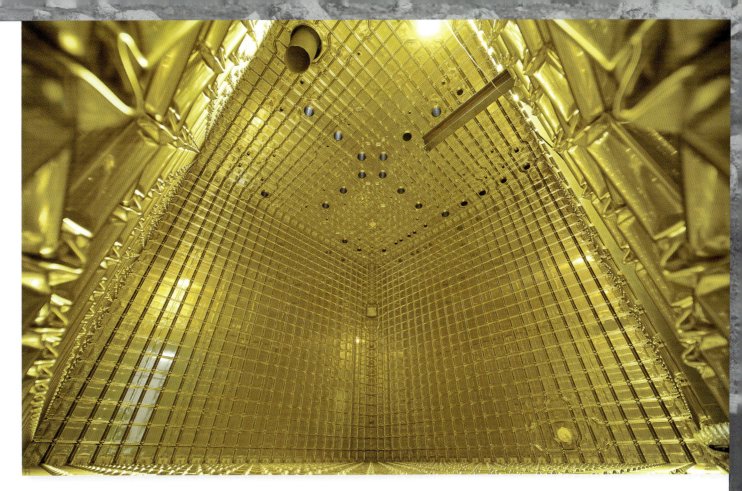

Stanford University and Fermilab,
Deep Underground Neutrino Experiment (DUNE),
between Illinois and South Dakota,
2023

above: Still under construction, DUNE is the world's most powerful neutrino experiment, consisting of a beam (1,300 kilometres (800 miles) long) and two detectors. Despite this prototype being a big gold room, the luxurious and hyper-futuristic avant-garde aesthetic is entirely technological, scientific, epistemic, materialist, ontological and metaphysical, being designed to discover the fundamentals of matter and the deep history and evolution of the universe.

And whilst there are dangers and limits in overextending posthumanisms and multispecies relationality (lots of life and technology is there to kill and/or eat us – including our own selves, in cancer), there is also the danger of not extending it far enough for, as the present climate crisis suggests, the posthuman problem of the place-design of the planet is the most contemporary and urgent architectural project of all.

On the edge of the speculative and design fiction, posthuman architecture includes exo- (off-Earth) and xeno- (alien) architecture.[11] Implausibly, one of the most posthuman architectures can also be presently and proleptically defined as that which actively indexes the entire *umwelt* and sensorium of all the possible perceiving stakeholders of the architecture itself.

A Metagram of Posthuman Space and Spatial Design
The most intelligent and urgent questions to ask about space or architecture are therefore more about which type of posthumanism is being implicated, and about not just whether it is posthuman enough, but in which ways it could and should be more so. It is these kinds of questions that preoccupy all the contributors to this issue – from academia and practice, researching in disciplines from architecture, interiors, engineering, the digital, interaction, product and vehicle design, urbanism, philosophy, fashion, theory, history, art, journalism, museology/curation and space architecture in the US, Austria, the Netherlands, Italy and the UK. That each responded in unique ways to this ⌂ is a measure of relevance and possibilities of 21st-century posthuman architecture.

The issue is structured in a narrative sequence starting with a core of theories and design(s), moving though technologies and futures, with case studies and more realised design projects interspersed throughout. The posthuman focus of each one or two articles alternates between the bio-, techno- and more hybrid posthumanisms, for each to enrich and question its precedessor and successor essays. A starter of Jacopo Leveratto's five-step 'cookbook' for bio-posthuman design is served, peppered with a variety of recent projects. Alberto Fernández González and myself use the posthuman intelligence of AI to define the aesthetics of posthuman architectures. From the B-Pro programmes at the Bartlett School of Architecture, University College London (UCL), Roberto Bottazzi, Tyson Hosmer and Mollie Claypool present the most recent and most posthuman student and research projects – demonstrating one of the fullest spectrums of posthuman design on the planet. Co-founder Ariane Lourie Harrison presents some of the most recent built projects from around the US of Harrison Atelier, one of the most explicitly posthuman teaching, research and professional offices. Focusing on the posthuman charm of fungi, Mario Carpo, Reyner Banham Professor of Architectural History and Theory at The Bartlett, historicises and theorises the digital entanglements of slime moulds into the architectural contemporary.

Professor and Chair of Fashion Studies at Columbia College Chicago Colbey Reid and Professor of Philosophy at York College of Pennsylvania Dennis Weiss extend their research on posthuman interiors into a critique of conventional digital technologies in the domestic realm with a series of artfully curated and surprising conclusions for our future posthuman residences, beyond simplistic 'smart homes'. Andrew Witt is Associate Professor in Practice of Architecture at Harvard University and co-founder of the Certain Measures design studio; his article concentrates on his built *Museum of the Future*, offering us a planetary posthuman *Wunderkammer* (cabinet of curiosities) of hybrid-high-tech and bio-posthumanisations. Sylvia Lavin, Professor of History and Theory of Architecture at Princeton University School of Architecture, goes back to the future by branching off with a case study of a cathectic apple tree – in a simultaneously prelapsarian, Modernist and ur-posthuman inverted *hortus conclusus* opening the posthuman in architecture then, for now, and always. We then land firmly in the zoological posthuman, with Bartlett lecturer Paul Dobraszczyk and architect and wildlife researcher Steven Hutt each taking fresh new perspectives on animal architectures. Whilst Dobraszczyk takes a hard and unblinking eye to the architectures of tame animals we farm and husband on lands around planet Earth, Hutt brings an eagle eye to the skies and 'flying-feral' aerial typologies.

Beyond the skies, beyond the Earth, a quartet of essays on space architectures completes this ⌂. Olga Bannova and

Virgo, European Gravitational Observatory, Cascina, Italy, 2017

One of the three new international interferometer laboratories that first proved the theory of gravitational waves in 2017 using laser beams housed in the two main 5-kilometre- (3-mile-) long axes seen in this aerial photograph of the observatory. This led to the new discipline of gravitational observation, recording historical evolutions of black holes and other galactic- and universal-scale phenomena and events. Gravity scientists and technologists are now more capable at researching and designing than architects, leading the design of and with the posthuman architectural fundamental of gravity in spatial design.

Notes
1. Rem Koolhaas, *The Countryside*, Taschen (Berlin), 2020, p 272.
2. Ihab Hassan, 'Prometheus as Performer: Toward a Postmodern Culture?', *The Georgia Review* 31, 1977, pp 830–50.
3. See, for example, Richard H Godden and Asa Simon Mittman (eds), *Monstrosity, Disability and the Posthuman in the Medieval and Early Modern World*, Palgrave Macmillan (Cham), 2019, and M David Litwa, *Posthuman Transformation in Ancient Mediterranean Thought*, Cambridge University Press (Cambridge), 2021.
4. See, for example, N Katherine Hayles, *How We Became Posthuman*, University of Chicago Press (Chicago, IL), 1999.
5. See Ewa Nowak, *Advancing the Human Self*, Peter Lang (Frankfurt), 2020, p 209.
6. Tamar Sharon, *Human Nature in an Age of Biotechnology: The Case for Mediated Posthumanism*, Springer (New York), 2013.
7. K Michael Hays, *Modernism and the Posthumanist Subject*, MIT Press (New York), 1992.
8. Nick Axel et al (eds), *Superhumanity: Design of the Self*, University of Minnesota Press (Minneapolis, MN), 2018.
9. Liam Young (ed), △ *Machine Landscapes: Architectures of the Post-Anthropocene*, January/February (no 1), 2019.
10. Andrés Jaque, Marina Otero Verzier and Lucia Pietroiusti (eds), *More-than-Human: A Reader*, Het Nieuwe Instituut (Waregem), 2021.
11. See Armen Avanessian et al, *Perhaps It Is High Time for a Xeno-architecture to Match*, Sternberg (Berlin), 2018.

Sandra Häuplick-Meusberger launch into a fleet of new space architectural projects in Europe and the US, and architecture firm Hassell's Xavier De Kestelier, Levent Ozruh and Jonathan Irawan present a previously unpublished and newly completed project for a new Moon base in collaboration with the European Space Agency. Space architect Brent Sherwood then contrasts posthuman space architectures against newly emerging terrestrial projects, for example by Blue Origin, of which he was previously Senior Vice President of Space Systems Development. My concluding epilogue essay projects into the future of posthuman spaceships and spacecraft with an analysis of the International Space Station and *Star Trek*'s Starship Enterprise.

Undermining/overmining this linear narrative, the issue spatialises a more complex design where disparate places, scales and disciplines strategically overlap around interiors, the urban, landscape, recent digital technologies and techniques. Micro-organisms are considered along with plants/trees and animals, and complex mixes of these in smaller microbiomes. The future of posthumanity through space architecture is also addressed through a speculative, techno-aesthetic analysis of two of the most developed posthuman architectures: the International Space Station (ISS) and the United Space Ship Enterprise (USSE).

Posthumanesque-Postarchitectural-Postfutures?

As a whole, this △ registers and presages some of the failures of human architecture at the scale of the planet (in many cases at the scale of the country and the city) as much as proposing more ameliorative posthumanising solutions. Ultimately posthuman architecture points to the idea that in some cases the not-just-human, the no-architect and no-architecture constitutes the ideal or optimal design act. After all, there have been six different species of hominin apart from *Homo sapiens* in the past 6 million years, and accelerating our own further extra-evolutionary development, architecture (with or without humans) will need to adapt. This also means – as we see with some agencies in this △ – architects learning to understand, design for and possibly even love the unlovable, ugly, boring, obtuse, repulsive, lethal or alien species, things and sites. More than AI or artificial life (AL), we need artificial generosity (AG), artificial kindness (AK), artificial justice (AJ), artificial wisdom (AW) and artificial love (AL) – concepts yet to feature in 21st-century architectural design (or digital) theories per se. Whilst the risks are high and the likely benefits now staples of speculative science and design fictions of the simplistic 'utopian' and 'sublime' clichés, the worst posthuman architecture will exceed any synthetic hells in which the 'post' indexes, inherits but exceeds the disasters of postmodernities. Posthuman architectures were not just always there, they are now the architectural everything, everywhere, and if not now then eventually and forever. △

Text © 2024 John Wiley & Sons Ltd. Images: pp 6–7 © Alexandr Chytil / Shutterstock; p 8(t) © Daniela Yaneva 2019; pp 8–9(b) © Alberto Fernández González and Mark Garcia, AI-generated images created using Midjourney; p 9(t) Mario Carpo, Mark Garcia and Steven Hutt; pp 10–11(b) ©Twin Peaks Productions, Inc, 2017; p 11(t) © Maximilien Brice/ CERN / Science Photo Library; pp 12–13 ©The Virgo Collaboration / CCO 1.0 / Science Photo Library

MORE-THAN–

A FIVE-STEP RECIPE FOR DECENTRING DESIGN

Jacopo Leveratto

–POST

```
Studio Other Spaces (Olafur Eliasson
and Sebastian Behmann),
Future Assembly,
Venice Architecture Biennale,
2021
```

Future Assembly responded to the invitation by Biennale curator Hashim Sarkis to imagine a United Nations inspired multilateral design. It was a radical response to the urgent, human-driven climate crisis, convening over 50 new planetary representatives.

The importance of a 'more-than-human' approach to architectural design is becoming ever clearer. While partly a response to global ecological disaster, this shift also reflects a recognition that design should not seek solely to solve human problems, but to create environments that facilitate emergent opportunities for a wide range of nonhuman occupants and processes. Jacopo Leveratto is based at the Politecnico di Milano, where he researches on radical forms of habitability and posthuman architecture. Here he describes five steps to achieving these aspirations.

Valentina Marcarini,
László,
MORE-THAN-POST,
Milan,
2023

'More-than-human' is not simply a catchy, freely adaptable design label; it embodies the natural and affirmative evolution of the posthuman stance. Through the intersection, transformation and abstraction of the elements of a more-than-human design approach, the poster outlines a tentative methodology in the form of an essential set of guidelines.

It might have been coincidental, or possibly not, but 2021 undeniably represented a notable turning point for the field of design – at least from a lexical standpoint. First, in January, a widely disseminated reader edited by Andrés Jaque, Lucia Pietroiusti and Marina Otero Verzier openly advocated for a relational approach of 'designing with' 'more-than-human' entities to expand the notion of cohabitation.[1] Subsequently, in May, the artist Olafur Eliasson responded to the Lebanese architect Hashim Sarkis's invitation to the Venice Biennale by issuing a More-than-Human Chart and calling upon more than 50 participants to form a Future Assembly focused on 'more-than-human stakeholders'.[2] Towards the end of June, a board of 18 experts – including architects like Kengo Kuma and Bjarke Ingels – presented to the European Commission the 'New European Bauhaus Concept Paper', which opened with the recommendation to designers to 'adopt a more-than-human … culture'.[3]

The paper thus sanctioned, from an institutional perspective, a concept that would subsequently be further developed by contributions to theory, such as Ron Wakkary's book on 'more-than-human centred worlds',[4] as well as by a constellation of outstanding practitioners. These included major offices like Studio Other Spaces and Office for Political Innovation, emerging practices like Studio Ossidiana and Atelier Dalziel, researchers and artists like Joyce Hwang and Alexandra Daisy Ginsberg, and nonprofit agencies such as the urban design studio Prostorož. All adopted the 'more-than-human' terminology originally introduced by the architect and researcher Stanislav Roudavski three years earlier to designate the creation of artificial habitats as substitutes for natural ones.[5] Within their context, the term was employed to characterise diverse efforts to shift the focus of design. These efforts, despite several declarations and manifestos, still struggle to form a more unified identity beyond being a collection of concerns and recurring themes.

Notes for a Cookbook

'More-than-human' is not only a catchy label, open to loose interpretation. On the contrary; from a theoretical perspective, it signifies a specific and recent development within a precise critical stance known as posthuman. This line of thinking, developed over the last 20 years, emerged through the gradual convergence of non-anthropocentric and post-humanistic theories, both of which reject the modern notion of 'man' as the interpretative limit of reality.[6] Today, reflecting heightened awareness of human impact on the planet's natural balance,[7] posthuman theory focuses on a biocentric perspective that recognises the entire living environment's inherent right to flourish, regardless of its instrumentality. This same concept, clarified by the affirmative use of the prefix 'post-', and which the term 'more-than-human' also refers to, aims to include, rather than exclude, human subjectivity within an expanded, technologically mediated continuum connecting nature and culture. It therefore urges architectural design to envision the world from the perspective of interspecies coexistence and collaboration. This not only introduces a new subject of reference in terms of fruition or agency, but also challenges the role of architects, planners and other practitioners in this field. In essence, it requires a holistic approach that acknowledges the entanglement of ecosystems, enabling the creation of spaces within which multiple species can find ways to cohabit. This challenge also involves providing methodological guidelines for translating 'post-' into 'more-than'. The set of principles presented here – developed after studying over 300 references, 200 paradigmatic examples and 20 case studies[8] – aims to address these challenges.

Studio Other Spaces (Olafur Eliasson and Sebastian Behmann), Future Assembly logo, Venice Architecture Biennale, 2021

Studio Other Spaces believed that envisioning potential futures requires designers to broaden their perceptions of coexistence and collaboration to include the more-than-human and to find novel ways of spatially representing diverse nonhuman agencies. To achieve this, they invited all Biennale participants to introduce more-than-human 'stakeholders' from their local contexts, to foster novel, imaginative ways to spatially depict diverse, nonhuman agencies.

Forget Solutions

The initial step in designing a more-than-human space is to consider its purpose. This, surprisingly, cannot in any way refer to 'solving a problem'. As the chemist and philosopher Isabelle Stengers wrote, the present historical moment is characterised by the impossibility of finding solutions for what she termed the 'intrusion of Gaia'.[9] This is because solutions tend to be incomplete, are usually focused on specific sectors, and can at times be ethically questionable. Furthermore, they imply a sense of control that, as perfectly elucidated by Michel Serres, is unrealistic when applied to complex systems like natural ones.[10] For instance, predicting the long-term consequences of reintroducing wild predators in urban areas to control specific pests is essentially impossible. Similarly, the retrospective realisation that efforts to promote urban beehives actually harmed native pollinators highlights the complexity of such interactions. This is why, instead of seeking solutions, Stengers proposed envisioning 'objectors' to the prevailing concept of development. These 'objectors' would focus on exploring connections not by directly producing outcomes, but through the 'production of repercussions'.[11] This is also why contemporary designers adopting a more-than-human approach prefer to devise projects that do not concentrate on nature-based solutions. Instead, they aim to increase architecture's receptivity to biological diversity by simply accommodating it, without any other underlying purpose.

Ultimately, the essence of designing more-than-human spaces – whether urban reserves, reintroduction colonies or platforms of exchange – should transcend the mere construction of functional habitats for other species. It predominantly involves augmenting the built environment's suitability for life and expanded forms of interspecies cohabitation. This, in turn, implies enhancing its permeability, multiplying and diversifying potential ecological niches, enabling novel relationships to develop organically beyond any predetermined hierarchies, and, naturally, accepting the inherent possibility of failure within this process.

Please, Do Disturb

Once the project's objective is clarified, the subsequent phase is to devise a strategic approach for intervention. However, there is the risk of misconstruing the act of accommodating other species as a mere retreat from constructive efforts. On the contrary, as observed by anthropologist Anna Tsing, the resurgence of nature often needs a human-triggered 'disturbance to enhance diversity and the healthy functioning of ecosystems'.[12] This principle extends to a specific kind of design – be it implemented by confinement or exclusion, augmentation or grafting – which, from a more-than-human perspective, does not exclude humanity and its formative role, but simply adjusts it by both giving validity to its position and displacing its centrality.

The concept of disturbance acknowledges not only the necessity of design, in most cases, to initiate the process of making space for more-than-human entities, but also the fact that, whatever its initial intentions, design frequently results in unintended effect. For this reason, designers in this field have begun regarding their actions not as fixed responses to specific programmes, but as catalysts or activating devices for new and unforeseen developments. Within the realm of design, this perspective considers projects as proposals, rather than as leading to predetermined outcomes. It occasionally even relinquishes the final responsibility of formalisation in favour of other forms of agency. This is not due to deliberate informality, but to the awareness that, when dealing with interspecies relationships, design outcomes are largely unpredictable. The essence of their quality lies not solely in their specific formal configuration, but in the nature of the invitation they extend, the diverse applications they accommodate, and the multiple opportunities for engagement they offer to heterogeneous inhabitants.

Studio Ossidiana,
The Seeds' Garden,
Shenzhen Bi-City Biennale
of Urbanism\Architecture,
Shenzhen, China,
2022–23

Here, the architects converted the former cistern of a Shenzhen brewery into a circular garden to be seeded and cultivated by birds and people. Visitors on a suspended walkway were invited to seed the field below, while birds, attracted by a series of sculptural feeders inspired by the architecture of barns, silos and ships' masts, fertilised the ground with their guano.

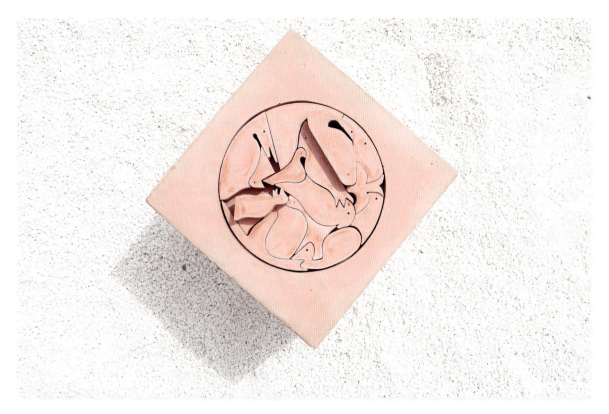

Studio Ossidiana,
Design for Utomhusverket,
Swedish Centre for Architecture
and Design (ArkDes),
Stockholm, Sweden,
2021

Studio Ossidiana envisioned a collective platform for encounters between people, plants, birds and minerals, devised as a vast garden-map, within which the public realm acted as a stage for intimate moments and public performance. The temporary field-gardens of Exercisplan incorporated a groundscape where shells, loam, water and gravel intersected to create new soils that could be shaped by digging, walking, reclining and playing.

Fortunately, the process of design is collaborative effort, and the very brief history of endeavours involving more-than-human entities includes a truly extraordinary collection of stories of mutual survival, scientific exchanges and ecological animism

Stay With and Make Kin

At this juncture, the tactical challenge of choosing the means of intervention entails confronting its specific context. When it comes to spaces involving more-than-human species, the complexity increases. These spaces not only host heterogeneous communities whose dynamics are even more difficult to understand than the behaviour of individual organisms, but these communities are also actively engaged in constructing their own habitats, as this capacity for habitat construction 'is not limited to humans' but belongs to 'all organisms [that] make ecological living places'.[13] Amid a confluence of projects that frequently overlap, collide or provide leeway for other actors, a complex and sometimes inadvertent process of shaping a multispecies milieu unfolds. This necessitates a shift in perspective, where these spaces are acknowledged as products of, and intended for, what Donna Haraway terms 'sympoietic' existences.[14] This, in turn, asks designers to attain a contextual understanding that eludes abstraction.

To consider other species, designers must think from their standpoint and immerse themselves in their world, irrespective of the potential for conflict within this relationship. Fortunately, the process of design is collaborative, and the very brief history of endeavours involving more-than-human entities includes a truly extraordinary collection of stories of mutual survival, scientific exchanges and ecological animism. Additionally, there exists extensive documentation that goes beyond conventional records and encompasses overlapping cartographies of avian migratory patterns, intricate cross-sectional depictions of root structures and geological strata, calendars of bloom periods, compendia of microbial life, narratives, interviews and manifestos – to name just a few. All of these and more emerged from motives having nothing to do with control, but rather with the aim of harmonising as many trajectories as possible and inciting reactions through projects.

When Undecided, Go Third

How to effectively intersect these trajectories is not merely another tactical concern, but one of paramount significance. A comprehensive grasp of this matter hinges on recognising, as does the philosopher Rosi Braidotti, that a contextually rooted understanding is operative only if it is coupled with the pursuit of novel frameworks that conceive of a subject as a dynamic and interconnected entity.[15] An example is Haraway's 'cyborg', or philosopher Gilles Deleuze's concept of the 'nomad', along with other fictional characters that, in the history of posthuman thought, have been used to express the rejection of binary identities in favour of complex singularities in their evolutionary course. These same conceptual frameworks, which have been developed since the architect and gardener Gilles Clément's time,[16] have found expression in the field of design through a rich catalogue of 'third spaces', characterised by their indeterminate, perpetually evolving nature. These spaces remain receptive to multiple forms of cross-fertilisation, shaped, on the one hand, by unconstrained patterns of natural growth and, on the other, by a meticulous acknowledgement of their biological imperative. They embody an expanded threshold wherein practices, relationships and notions of existence develop freely. At present this challenges the conventional typological cataloguing within which dwelling projects are usually confined, by reassessing the subjectivity that lies at its core. Such reassessment calls for a conceptual shift, such as contemplating programmes in terms of interconnectivity rather than division, openness rather than segregation, and indeterminacy instead of specialisation. Yet, it might be achieved by the simple act of regarding architecture as a distinct form of collaborative creation, underpinned by the affirmative notion of radical inclusion – encompassing humans, other creatures, flora, technologies, microorganisms and beyond – which is already implicit in a more-than-human worldview.

Make No Rooms But Resonance Chambers

Finally, when embarking on the design of a more-than-human habitat, there is one lingering misconception to dispel before beginning to draw. The ideas of openness and indeterminacy outlined here might erroneously imply that the configuration of these spaces, or the activating mechanisms within them, is of minor relevance. Quite the opposite holds true: numerous contemporary endeavours within the field challenge the prevailing doctrine that champions an eco-scientific approach to systems and metabolisms, to restore an idea of architecture as a historically constituted symbolic system. From a certain perspective, akin to any other reconstructive reading of nature, they complicate 'the claim' – as architectural historian David Gissen has written – 'that contemporary ecological, bio-mimetic, and geo-mimetic work operates in a post-representational regime'.[17] They advance an architectural interpretation that, while acknowledging the intricate web of systemic processes and exchanges involved, shifts emphasis away from physical interrelations to focus on distinct formal archetypes and their intrinsic symbolic potency. Through this lens, they present their projects poetically; not solely as sets of instructions for living outside the norm, but rather as genuine and attainable, socially acceptable 'promises of happiness' – however limited our comprehension of the happiness of other species might be.[18] These pledges are woven of seeds and abodes, plazas and woodlands; they speak the language of ravines and clouds, nutrient streams and Arcadian visions. While possibly utopian and, admittedly, far from being perfect – at least from an operational point of view, given their inherent susceptibility to setbacks – they collectively make up an array of what Stengers defines as 'resonance chambers'.[19] They challenge the prevailing human-centric perspective by illustrating how biodiversity, for instance, can embody not only a scientific concept, but may also represent the most beautiful way of inhabiting the world that one may imagine. ⌑

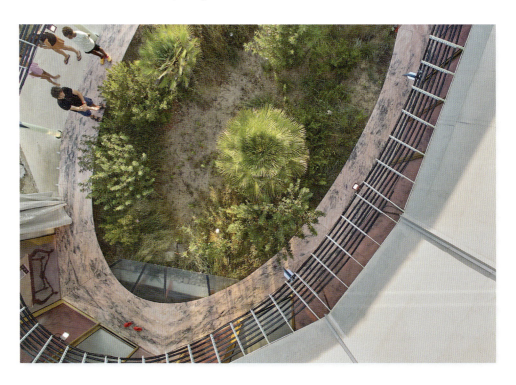

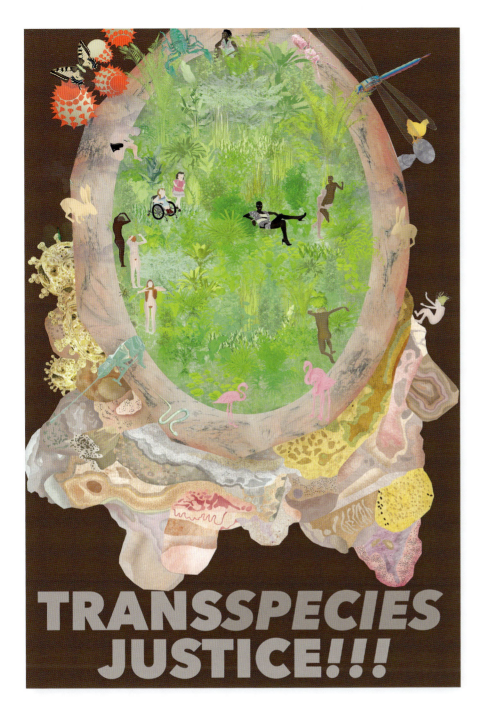

Notes
1. Andrés Jaque, Marina Otero Verzier and Lucia Pietroiusti, *More-Than-Human*, Het Nieuwe Instituut (Rotterdam), 2021.
2. https://futureassembly.earth.
3. New European Bauhaus High-Level Round Table (Shigeru Ban et al), 'New European Bauhaus Concept Paper', 30 June 2021: https://new-european-bauhaus.europa.eu/system/files/2021-07/2021-06-30_New_European_Bauhaus_Concept_Paper_HLRT_FINAL.pdf.
4. Ron Wakkary, *Things We Could Design: For More Than Human-Centered Worlds*, MIT Press (Cambridge, MA), 2021.
5. Stanislav Roudavski, 'Notes on More-than-Human Architecture', in Gretchen Coombs, Andrew McNamara and Gavin Sade (eds), *Undesign*, Routledge (London), 2018, pp 24–37.
6. Rosi Braidotti, *The Posthuman*, Polity (Cambridge), 2013.
7. Paul J Crutzen, 'Geology of Mankind', *Nature* 415, 2002, p 23.
8. Jacopo Leveratto, *Posthuman Architectures: A Catalogue of Archetypes*, ORO (Novato, CA), 2021.
9. Isabelle Stengers, *In Catastrophic Times: Resisting the Coming Barbarism*, Open Humanities Press (Lüneburg), 2015, p 41.
10. Michel Serres, *Le Contrat naturel*, Flammarion (Paris), 1992.
11. Stengers, *op cit*, p 24.
12. Anna Lowenhaupt Tsing, *The Mushroom at the End of the World: On the Possibility of Life in Capitalist Ruins*, Princeton University Press (Princeton, NJ), 2015, p 152.
13. *Ibid*, p 22.
14. Donna J Haraway, *Staying With the Trouble: Making Kin in the Chthulucene*, Duke University Press (Chicago, IL), 2016, p 58.
15. Braidotti, *op cit*, pp 163–9.
16. Gilles Clément, *Manifeste du Tiers paysage*, Éditions Sujet/Objet (Paris), 2003.
17. David Gissen, 'The Architectural Reconstruction of Nature', in Stan Allen and Marc McQuade (eds), *Landform Building: Architecture's New Terrain*, Lars Müller (Zürich), 2011, p 456.
18. Leveratto, *op cit*, p 210.
19. Stengers, *op cit*, pp 152–3.

Andrés Jaque / Office for Political Innovation and Miguel Mesa del Castillo, Rambla Climate-House, Molina de Segura, Murcia, Spain, 2021

opposite: The house was designed as an ecological device to restore the biodiversity of Murcia's territorial system of ravines *(ramblas)*, as part of a series of associated initiatives to mitigate and repair the environmental damage caused by local over-urbanisation. It is organised around an elliptical section of *rambla*, as a sequence of interconnected spaces of different widths, acting as an observatory in harmony with the reconstructed landscape.

above: Concept poster. After the restoration of the rambla's hydro-thermal environment, its previous more-than-human inhabitants have re-emerged only one year later. *Brachypodiums*, myrtles, mastic trees, fan palms, oleanders and flame trees (*Brachychiton acerifolius*) have begun to grow in the elliptical section, while insects, birds and lagomorphs use it for shelter.

Text © 2024 John Wiley & Sons Ltd. Images: pp 14–15, 17 © 2021 Studio Other Spaces; p 16 © Valentina Marcarini; pp 18–19 © Studio Ossidiana; pp 20–21 © Andrés Jaque / Office for Political Innovation + Miguel Mesa del Castillo

Alberto Fernández González
and Mark Garcia

A Posthuman Architectural Artificial Intelligence *Speculum?*

Alberto Fernández González,
PostHuman City 2123: Between Earth and Mars,
Posthuman AIchitectural Speculations,
2023

A titanic pseudo-organic orbital, growing in several directions and in which the multi-posthuman agents and ecologies traverse the cityscape under a dynamic multi-gravity regime. A megastructural ballet of an AI-negotiated future posthuman city.

Text and Images in Future Spaces

The long-term research project Posthuman AIchitectural Speculations is a collaboration between **Alberto Fernández González and Mark Garcia**, both of whom are lecturers at the Bartlett School of Architecture, University College London, and PhD candidates on the Architecture and Digital Theory programme there. Here they investigate how well artificial intelligence can help develop posthuman architectures and the symbiotic relationship between language and AI as a way of speculating about spatial futures.

How much do and how can artificial intelligences learn about and contribute to posthuman architecture as design, aesthetics, form, style, topology and geometry? How well do AI image generators understand posthuman architectures, and what is the value of their productions? How can they represent and help us research, speculate and integrate posthuman concepts and technologies into future architectures? These questions are addressed in this article through the process and partial product of the research project Posthuman AIchitectural Speculations. The project investigates the current historical, theoretical and speculative-futurological aspects and values of AI-generated architectural images of posthuman spaces and spans historical, pre- and non-modern designed spaces (including in landscapes and interiors through their depictions in 17th-century Western oil paintings), architectures, spacecrafts and posthuman cities.

The development of AI image generators has led to a surge in emotive and dramatic debates within global architectural media and discourse. These discussions often feature extravagant utopian (eg 'The Hyper-Intelligent Architect') and dystopian (eg the 'AI Murder of the Architect') AIs, with shockingly short time frames of three to five years projected for these scenarios.[1] Utilising posthuman AI to investigate spatial design issues presents a pragmatic, empirical and projectively appropriate primary and design research method. These aims are, in a strong sense, both absurd and impossible – how and why could and should a single epistemic and synecdochic image encapsulate the vast numbers and types of posthuman architectural spaces? Despite its implausibility, artists, designers, advertisers and curators as much as art historians employ this 'case-study' scholarly method. Art historian William John Thomas Mitchell in *Image Science* (2018)[2] refers to these types of images as 'metapictures', though in this case, the preferred term is 'metagrams'. As the research project progressed, further questions arose around the minimum and maximum quantities of information and guidance input that would be required for the AI to generate outputs that either resemble possible realities or existing images of posthuman architectures and spaces and about which types of prompts (text, images or both – the 'trilectic method') yield the most successful results.

Image-Posthumanising/Posthuman-Imaging Metagrams/Softwares
After conducting ad-hoc experimentation with various AI image generators including Midjourney, Dall-e2 and Stable Diffusion, it was decided to utilise the last one as the primary image generation tool and DiffusionBee as the designated diffuser within this framework. The decision was based on Stable Diffusion's superior performance in generating high-quality, coherent images that aligned with the project's architectural research goals and the use of general processing units (GPUs) completely detached from the cloud (keeping the integrity of the research while adhering to intellectual property regulations). This workflow enabled the production of a diverse and imaginative collection of AI-generated images that not only showcased a wide range of posthuman architectural styles but also pushed the boundaries of traditional architectural design. The collaboration between the AI tools and the research

Alberto Fernández González and Mark Garcia,
Posthuman Architecture + Insects,
Posthuman AIchitectural Speculations,
2023

AIs can produce uncanny and sometimes monstrous (both good and bad) representations of speculative biology and alien or genetically designed zooforms. Scientists and researchers are researching and designing mergers of robotics, AIs and insects. Some posthumanisms ask how arthropods might be designed for in new architectures which might exclude humans or as co-residents with them and other posthuman agents.

team allowed for a unique exploration of the potentials and limitations of AI-generated imagery in the context of architecture.

This study focuses on eight metagrams of posthuman architectures, contextualised by their adjacent disciplinary types of dataset spaces. The analysis bypasses Modernisms and Postmodernisms to introduce a historical element. The six datasets include 'Posthuman Cities', 'Premodern and Non-Modern Posthuman Architectures', 'Posthuman Interiors', 'Posthuman Spacecraft/Spaceship Architectures' and 'Posthuman Spacecraft/Spaceship'.

An initial test-design prompted by 'Posthuman Architecture' yielded a highly abstracted result. This premature outcome drew from a curated set of 89 images, consisting of drawings, renderings, photographs and models of both built and unbuilt posthuman architectural case studies (including posthuman architectures identified by other academics and architects).[3]

To supplement the visual material/prompts,[4] a grouped hierarchy of 114 terms was derived from an ongoing thematic and multimedia mediagraphic analysis of concepts that characterise or operationalise posthumanisms in the 21st century (1999–present).[5] These terms have been cross-verified through over 500 separate multidisciplinary and mediagraphic items, encompassing posthuman spaces, architectures, designs, technologies, theories and philosophies.

A predictive, prospective, speculative and proleptic element was introduced through proxies for the 'futurological' aspects of posthuman theories and philosophies. These proxies were drawn from science fiction, cinema, television, literature, contemporary art and new media.

As a rapid study case, one key image input was a photograph[6] of the newly built vault (completed 2010) in Antoni Gaudí's Sagrada Família basilica, Barcelona. This structure serves as an exemplary transhistorical architectural project, showcasing both the symbiosis and synthesis of its formal and tectonic organism as well as its technological genesis and construction. Textual prompts were also incorporated into the design process.

Finally, by examining the eight metagrams of posthuman architectures, this study provides a comprehensive understanding of the evolving spatial design landscape. The analysis not only highlights the diverse range of posthuman architectural styles but also underscores the importance of historical context and adjacent disciplinary types in shaping future architectural discourse.

Posthumanisms to Concepts/Texts/Words

The role of language in posthuman architectural design was examined in this research through a focus on the interplay between text, words and images across six key datasets – one for each main image target sought. Each dataset was prompted by a custom set of approximately 20 unique terms generated from the thematic analysis of posthuman theories and philosophies in the extant English-language literature. Ordered into a hierarchy sequence, these terms were weighted to include key disciplines, practice domains, case-study examples, dominant programme/functional types, and enabling technologies and media distilled from the initial set of 114 terms (though some single-word prompts needed prefixing with additional contextual and situational terms like 'space' to narrow their specificity). To complement the textual data, a refined set of five to ten images unique to each dataset was also used, drawn from the authors' PhD mediagraphies primarily in the design disciplines.

The study focused on case studies and terms that demonstrated as many posthuman indicators in concepts, elements and technologies as possible. Images were likewise ranked in a sequence hierarchy, with some level of negotiated intersubjective and relative judgment involved.

By examining the relationship between language and posthuman architectural design, this study highlights the importance of text, words and images in shaping the future of spatial design. The analysis provides valuable insights into the interplay between posthumanism and language, emphasising the significance of interdisciplinary perspectives in advancing architectural discourse.

Alberto Fernández González and Mark Garcia,
Transhistorical Organo-AI Posthuman Interior,
Posthuman AIchitectural Speculations,
2023

This structure morphs an interior photograph by Alberto Fernández González of the new parts of Antoni Gaudí's Sagrada Família, one of the most innovative, transhistorical and large-scale syntheses of digital and biomorphic posthuman architectures. Gaudí's design, begun in the 19th century, has been augmented with new posthuman technologies that are co-authored with the computer into a spatial historiographical narrative of life and growth in time that unfolds with each architectural detail.

Alberto Fernández González and Mark Garcia,
Pre-human and Non-Human Future Landscapes and
Designed Posthuman Biological Architectures,
Posthuman AIchitectural Speculations,
2023

In both pre-human and posthuman landscapes, agents and organisms become blurred. Some theories of posthuman AI aim to dismantle the distinctions between nature and culture, creating a fusion of deliberate design and unintentional hybrids with nonhuman elements. Is it possible that posthuman architecture resembles the pre-human, non-modern and historical representations of spaces?

Conceptions/Results: Primary and Secondary Metagrams

When the text prompt 'posthuman' was input into various AI image generation software, the majority of results were portraits of sci-fi-styled cyborgian humanoids with minor technological prosthetic implants. These images were generally non-photorealistic headshots. The process then advanced to the next level of architectural-based prompts in the prompt hierarchy.

The AI-generated images predominantly featured generic late-Modernist and commercial-looking digital architectures, with little evidence of Postmodernism or advanced technology. Most images appeared as illustrations, sometimes hand-drawn, and lacked resolution, detail or further development. Consequently, the terms 'hyperrealistic' and 'hyperreal' were added to the text prompts, leading to the generation of more lifelike images.

Finally, analysis of outputs from the first phase of the research reveals the challenges in producing AI-generated posthuman architectural imagery that is both realistic and technologically advanced. The study underscores the importance of refining text prompts to enhance the quality and relevance of the generated images, contributing to the ongoing exploration of AI's role in architectural design and representation.

In AI-generated content, the problem of sequentially chaining prompts poses challenges in creating coherent and synthesised outputs. It arises when multiple input prompts are provided in a sequence and the AI is expected to generate a coherent set of images based on these prompts. However, instead of synthesising the images in a way that takes into account the entire sequence, the AI often generates disjointed outputs that may lack coherence when viewed together. This issue can be attributed to limitations in the AI's understanding and processing of context when dealing with multiple prompts – a problem of continuing relevance outside the scope of this article.

In the context of posthuman architectural design, the list of prompts evolved sequentially from single concepts to whole sentences and paragraphs, each addressing different spatial dimensions of posthumanism. A more complex 'natural language' generator prompt for the 'Posthuman City' image-hypothesis was therefore then designed and tested to address the challenge of sequentially chaining prompts in AI-generated content. Utilising all the previous prompts from phase 1, a 375-word text was composed (produced in ChatGPT) as a final text prompt (in the form of a natural-language description of a posthuman city) which included all the previous single-word prompts.

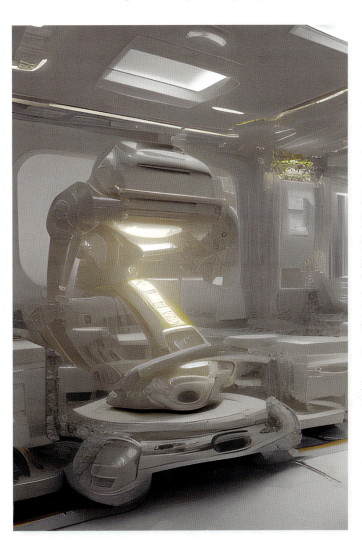

Alberto Fernández González and Mark Garcia,
Phase 2 Posthuman Synthesis,
Posthuman AIchitectural Speculations,
2023

In this phase of the research, thousands of images generated by the complete set of textual and image-based prompts were input into Midjourney and resulted in paradoxically plausible-seeming, increasingly abstracted but recognisably modern architectures. Often of epic scale but predominantly occupied by oddly carefully integrated plant life and frequently including more futuristic, small-scale and complex architectural elements, these are of unknown typologies and functions.

Alberto Fernández González and Mark Garcia,
Posthuman Interior: Robotic,
Posthuman AIchitectural Speculations,
2023

A key driver of technology-oriented posthumanisms is robotics and automation. As humans co-adapt and cohabit with increasingly automated and robotic spaces as well as independent and increasingly intelligent robots, interior design is being influenced by a more developed and extended common design language found currently in embryonic stage in some well-designed vehicles, spacecraft and parametric architectures.

The Posthuman *Speculum Maius*?

The present study has explored the rapidly evolving landscape of AI-generated posthuman architectural imagery, examining the challenges and potential of incorporating AI image generators in architectural design and research. The investigation revealed the unpredictable and nonlinear nature of AI-driven co-design, blurring the distinctions between human and AI into a posthuman assemblage.

Future research should focus on utilising more diverse and inclusive historical precedents, including large-scale international and multicultural datasets, to better distinguish the posthuman from adjacent concepts such as post-digital, postmodern and post-industrial. Moreover, refining the prompts to encompass synonyms for 'posthuman' can further enhance the AI's understanding and spatialisation of posthumanisms.

The AI architects of the next century will need to identify and manage significant and innovative spatial design problems and research projects rather than undertake or answer them alone. The challenge for senior and advanced academic and professional leaders in global architectural research is to formulate research questions that are excellent, wise and kind enough to drive the field forward. Those unable to imagine or address these questions or find suitable collaborators (human, nonhuman or AI) will see the work done for or without them.

The experience of co-designing with AIs was often a matter of highly unpredictable, nonlinear, rapid, savant-like progress and proliferation. At times, it seemed to stagnate or even regress and degenerate in its ability to advance, with diminishing and even retrogressive returns on the sophistication of its spatialisation of posthumanisms. The logics of the plausible genealogies of the patterns of posthumanisms became unrecognisable. Despite moments of clarity and comprehension, the AI's outputs eccentrically con-fused and be-wildered detailing, per-mutating these across figure–ground, object–context and subject–object.

Alberto Fernández González and Mark Garcia,
Posthuman Interior: Factory,
Posthuman AIchitectural Speculations,
2023

above: The 21st century is producing new posthuman scales and types of factories, and this will only intensify throughout the Fourth Industrial Revolution and Third Machine Age, defining one key mutation of posthuman architectures with minimal human 'in-person' presences.

Alberto Fernández González and Mark Garcia,
Premodern and Non-Modern Posthuman Interior: Ecology,
Posthuman AIchitectural Speculations,
2023

opposite: Artificial mountainous ecologies at the scale of landscapes are fictional concepts, such as the orbital 'Bernal spheres' proposed by US physicist Gerard K O'Neil in the mid-1970s; but enclosed biomes updating John P Allen's Biosphere 2 in Arizona (1991) and Grimshaw Associates' Eden Project in Cornwall, UK (2000) are increasingly possible, featuring for instance in the multi-generational interstellar spaceships envisioned by the joint Defence Advanced Research Projects Agency (DARPA) and NASA '100 Year Starship' initiative.

This hyperplenitude inevitably caused egregious errors in trials in form-and-function relationships, and often derailed the project's progress, resulting in seemingly self-sabotaging and ridiculous representations of posthuman space. However, the AI's unselfconscious, efflorescent and rampant aesthetic preferences blurred the lines between this new co-emergent human–AI posthuman assemblage, entangling computer, software, image and text into semi-auto black-boxed design systems and networks. Consequently, new architectural and spatial design tests, such as Turing, Feigenbaum, Swirski, Hernández-Orallo and Dowe tests, will be needed to analyse and better understand this enigmatic agency, its creations and their significance. The next phases of this ongoing research project will involve investigating and interpreting these images in 3D and 4D for further theoretical elaboration. Architecture urgently needs an Arch-AI to generate 3D (depth-mapped) architectures but with additional integrated physics engine and gravity simulator, and finite element analysis (FEA) for structural engineering, to deliver plausible architectures and not just risible, empty images of architecture.

In conclusion, the rapidly evolving field of AI-generated posthuman architectural imagery presents both challenges and opportunities for architects and researchers. By addressing the limitations of current AI systems and refining the input prompts, the future of architectural design may witness a seamless integration of AI-driven creativity and innovation, ultimately redefining the boundaries of human–AI collaboration. Embracing this posthuman future, we must ask ourselves: what do we imagine for the spectacle of space and the space of the spectacle, and how will we contribute architecturally and spatially to this heterotopic 21st-century *Speculum Maius* (the title, meaning *Great Mirror*, that the 13th-century friar Vincent of Beauvais gave to his attempt at a compendium of all knowledge available at the time)? Viewed as a true 'Great Mirror', it reflects the essence of our development, using latent spaces as the glass through which we may explore and seek answers to our yet unknown questions. ᗐ

Notes
1. Neil Leach, 'Tell Me AI Ain't Scary: AI and the Death of the Architect', 13 January 2023: https://www.youtube.com/watch?v=5eLMSYgHuuE; see also Neil Leach, *Architecture in the Age of Artificial Intelligence*, Bloomsbury (London), 2021.
2. WJT Mitchell, *Image Science*, University of Chicago Press (Chicago, IL), 2018.
3. Mark Garcia, Various figures from Digital Archive 'The 21st Century Posthuman Architectural Design of Spaceships and Spacecraft, PhD thesis in progress', University College London, 2023.
4. *Ibid*.
5. *Ibid*. Extracted from 'Chapter 2: Posthuman Theories and Philosophies'.
6. Taken by Alberto Fernández González.

Text © 2024 John Wiley & Sons Ltd. Images: pp 22–3 © Alberto Fernández González 2023, AI-generated image created using Stable Diffusion; pp 25–9 © Alberto Fernández González and Mark Garcia, AI-generated images created using Stable Diffusion

Roberto Bottazzi, Tyson Hosmer and Mollie Claypool

DISRU ECOLO DESIGN WITH INTELLIGENC

```
Jiwen Bian, Trishla Chadha, Rajita Jain and Zhaoyi Wang,
Mood-ulated Subtopia,
B-Pro Urban Design RC14,
Bartlett School of Architecture,
University College London (UCL),
London,
2022
```

Mood-ulated Subtopia employs machine-learning methods to map and design the emotive and perceptual aspects of urban navigation. The design proposes a soft urbanism built around ephemeral, qualitative aspects such as lighting and colour to provide a more diverse experience of the public space. (RC14 is directed by Roberto Bottazzi and Tasos Varoudis and supported by Eirini Tsouknida, Margarita Chaskopoulou and Vasileios Papalexopoulos.)

PTIVE
GIES
NONHUMAN
ES

In the last decade, the B-Pro post-professional Architectural Design Master's programmes in Architectural Design (AD) and Urban Design (UD) at the Bartlett School of Architecture, University College London have developed innovative research delving into various aspects of design and digital technologies. Such preoccupations include biotechnology, computation and artificial intelligence, digital fabrication and robotics. Programme directors **Roberto Bottazzi and Tyson Hosmer, and** Theory Coordinator **Mollie Claypool**, illustrate some of its recent thought-provoking work.

The urgent challenges posed by the climate crisis, resource depletion and housing shortages demand the adoption of innovative ecological approaches in architecture and urban design while artificial intelligence (AI), robotics and smart technologies are radically reshaping how we design, construct and co-inhabit buildings and cities with nonhuman participants. Technologist James Bridle's book *Ways of Being: Beyond Human Intelligence* (2022)[1] challenges our conventional understanding of intelligence, urging us to embrace nonhuman perspectives and question anthropocentric models. Posthuman architecture enables us to address our pressing responsibilities, creating adaptive, sustainable, inclusive built environments that negotiate the complex needs of humans, AI, machines and other nonhuman intelligences.

At the Bartlett School of Architecture, University College London, B-Pro[2] (Bartlett Prospective) – directed by Professor Frédéric Migayrou – brings together five graduate programmes, including Architectural Design (AD) and Urban Design (UD). With a unique research-driven approach, B-Pro operates at the intersection of advanced design, architecture and urbanism with state-of-the-art technology and theory. Each Research Cluster (RC) has a unique focus, enabling students to collaborate with researchers and practitioners, developing architectural and urban projects that push the boundaries of design research.

Autonomous Architectural Ecologies
Our traditional notion of intelligence is synonymous with human intelligence. We must step beyond anthropocentric intelligence to radically reappraise the viewpoint from which we develop architecture. Bridle describes our need as a species to discover an 'ecology of technology', forming new relationships with technology and nonhuman intelligences to live with the world, rather than seeking to dominate it. We have the responsibility to shift the architectural paradigm from the design of static buildings only considered by and for humans towards an ecological viewpoint where design is conducted as and for adaptive architectural ecosystems with other nonhuman intelligences.

Faizunsha Ibrahim Ghousiaa, Eric Hughes, Sergio Eduardo Mutis and Lia Papoutsi,
Diffusive Habitats,
B-Pro Architectural Design RC3,
Bartlett School of Architecture,
University College London (UCL),
London,
2022

Diffusive Habitats is an autonomous reconfigurable architecture with an adaptive building life cycle that adjusts its spatial configuration through a multi-user platform. The research integrates agent-based spatial planning with reinforcement learning with a distributed robotic material system with reversible timber blocks. The robotic system is developed with bi-directional cyber-physical control trained through deep reinforcement learning in a simulator to optimise collaborative decision-making assembly strategies. (RC3 is directed by Tyson Hosmer, Octavian Gheorghiu and Philipp Siedler and supported by Ziming He, Baris Erdincer and Panagiotis Tigas.)

The AD programme's interdisciplinary approach is both scientific and speculative, providing an open platform for Research Clusters to develop innovative ecologies of technology addressing critical issues of our present and future world. This selection of research and projects illustrates investigations into new forms of architectural agency through posthuman themes including designing with nonhuman intelligences, living with autonomous machines, platforms with AI agents, territorial-scale ecological design, and designing for and living with biological material systems.

How will autonomously adaptive robotic environments fundamentally change our way of living? RC3, titled Living Architecture Lab, develops 'living architecture' as a coupling of living systems with the continuous [re]formation of architecture. The lab holistically reappraises the unsustainable linear life cycles of buildings, learning from living systems' extraordinary scalable efficiencies of adaptive construction with simple flexible parts.

The research focuses on developing autonomously reconfigurable buildings integrating AI-driven generative design platforms, novel robotic material systems and cyber-physical simulation, sensing and control, enabling intelligent spatial adaptation with a continuous feedback chain. Experimental models are embedded with the ability to self-organise, self-assess and self-improve using deep reinforcement learning to train adaptive design algorithms and adaptive robotic assembly systems.

The research operates across scales and typologies, from collaborative robotic assembly and reconfiguration to adaptive robotic tensegrity to robotic spatial embodiment. Projects develop new socio-economic models and scalable platforms for distributed living, working and production. For example, a project from RC3 is Diffusive Habitats (2022), which expands the lab's posthuman research, envisioning continuously transformative architectural ecosystems shared by humans, intelligent computational agents, robots and modular building parts.

How can automation platforms with artificial intelligence be embedded in the design and inhabitation of housing?

Mindful of the social and political consequences of automation, RC4, AUAR Labs, develops community-driven platforms for homes and housing using automated workflows, with real-time feedback from both human and nonhuman agents for the assembly, configuration and reconfiguration of living spaces. Utilising discrete design and fabrication technologies, the research is set in the present, while being invested in radical spatial and aesthetic agendas for the future. The work investigates community, work, life and domesticity in an increasingly automated world.

The lab's research has tackled a range of posthuman topics, from life with robots to design platforms with AI. RC4's project YIMBY (Yes In My Back Yard) (2022) is an AI-driven platform helping self-builders to densify their own communities. The toolkit enables citizens to use their own assets, taking ownership and ultimately the development of their communities into their own hands. The planning process uses machine learning to negotiate programme, typology and tectonics while a mobile robotic factory assembles modular timber building blocks on site, which are then assembled by self-builders.

Mengzhen Guo, Yusong Hu, Jingwei Li and Yangzhi Li, YIMBY (Yes In My Back Yard), B-Pro Architectural Design RC4, Bartlett School of Architecture, University College London (UCL), London, 2022

The YIMBY (Yes In My Back Yard) platform serves as a collective toolbox to empower self-builders to densify and redefine their own communities, leveraging machine learning to negotiate programme, typology and tectonics. An intriguing high-density version of the typical English suburb emerges, questioning what is shared and what is public. (RC4 is directed by Gilles Retsin, Manuel Jiménez García, Mollie Claypool and Kevin Saey and supported by David Doria and Sonia Magdziarz.)

Monumental Wastelands, RC1's title, explores posthumanism through two strands of research at architectural and territorial scales. The 'cli-migration' strand examines the forced migration of people due to climatic conditions, while the 'autonomous ecologies' strand addresses automation, rights and participation with nature. Strategies of preservation through adaptation embrace imminent realities rather than deny them, through methods of decoding and recoding.

Architecturally, this is achieved by dismantling and archiving existing buildings and their parts which are upcycled into new construction systems through participatory platforms. At territorial scales, ecological simulations are studied alongside environmental legislation to inform terraforming strategies. By choreographing land forming machines and natural processes with legal loopholes, human value systems that are imposed onto nature are reappropriated to enable its protection.

Narrative and climate-fiction through videogames and film are used to enter the perspectives of humans, nonhumans and machines serving as design feedback mechanisms. In RC1's project Gaming Consensus (2021), the film begins with an optimistically naïve tone towards gamification, taking a dark humorous turn that reveals the limitations of participatory design.

Finally, RC7, whose research title is Biospatial Design, challenges approaches to architecture which seek to separate the human from the nonhuman world. The research focuses on multi-species design approaches of building with living agencies to create cities that are sustainable, healthy and biodiverse.

The computational research utilises AI to remove anthropocentric bias, giving design agency to nonhuman participation through a procedural design framework that integrates eco-centric deep-learning models with biologically active materials and spaces. These methodologies leverage environmental and nonhuman data analytics within computational and material processes, resulting in biodiverse and material-focused buildings. Large-scale fabrication methods enable living building materials such as loofah, mycelium and plant roots to self-assemble

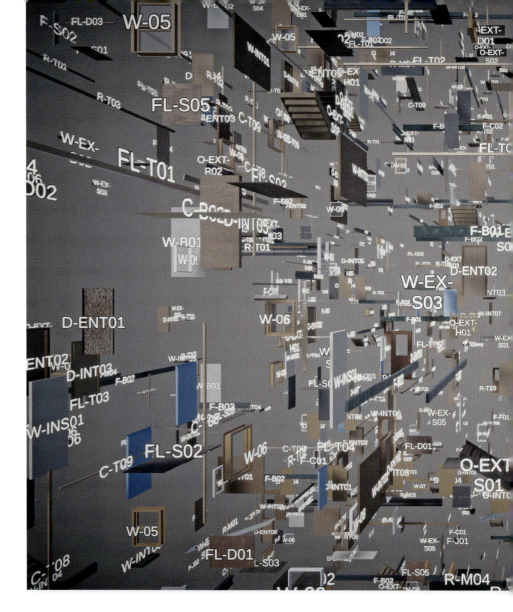

Junyi Du, Bingchuan Jiang, Beiyuan Zhang and Xiayi Zheng,
Gaming Consensus,
B-Pro Architectural Design RC1,
Bartlett School of Architecture,
University College London (UCL),
London,
2021

above: Gaming Consensus addresses the issue of a small indigenous coastal community in Kivalina, Alaska that will be flooded within five years due to rising sea levels. Having rejected all government relocation schemes, the project proposes a multi-player video game for participatory design to facilitate the negotiation of the various steps of the relocation process between community members, enabling the locals to self-dismantle, plan, relocate and redesign their future homes and town from their existing one. (RC1 is directed by Hadin Charbel and Déborah López Lobato and supported by Joris Putteneers.)

Yi Sui, Chris Whiteside and Zhan Xu,
More Than Human,
B-Pro Architectural Design RC7,
Bartlett School of Architecture,
University College London (UCL),
London,
2021

opposite: Through experimentation with procedural dataset design and generative neural networks, More Than Human has developed an eco-centric sketching tool that integrates both human and nonhuman spaces as lines are drawn. Simple human inputs are interpreted by a neural network and processed through a series of site-specific environmental analyses to produce a massing model with embedded ecological intelligence. The spatial programmes and bioreceptive forms that emerge are then driven towards the flourishing of multiple species. (RC7 is directed by Richard Beckett, Barry Wark and Levent Ozruh.)

through biological growth, while secondary living organisms are embedded for a range of health and environmental functions.

In the project More Than Human (2021), RC7 challenges the paradigm of building first and landscape second, considering a building as a holobiont construct, composed of a multitude of species, operating at multiple scales. Its design tool leverages procedural dataset design and neural networks that integrate human and nonhuman data to embed building tectonics with ecological intelligence.

Cities of Multiple Intelligences

As a discipline, urban design is in a peculiar position. On the one hand, urban migration increases the prominence of cities in conditioning people's life and environment; on the other, the discipline is stagnating, unable to update its design methods to conceive new approaches to unprecedented problems. Through the research developed in the different RCs, the B-Pro Urban Design (UD) mobilises computation to rethink design methods, agendas and aesthetics for urban life. Computation is an essential component acting as an instrument to navigate the epistemological uncertainties of urban environments, an enabler for different forms of intelligence to emerge and an infrastructure for exchange between human and nonhuman. The theoretical horizon animating the work draws from the posthumanist discourse to speculate on the urban impact of the climate emergency, planetary urbanism, the penetration of different forms of intelligence (living or in silico) and the economic and social transformations caused by technological innovation. Within this rich setup, some paradigmatic projects exemplify how the different research agendas in the B-Pro UD programme rethink urban design.

The work developed under the research theme of Hidden Dimensions by RC11 innovates the design process by engaging with the fundamental mathematical concepts underpinning computation. The potential of computers, in fact, does not lie solely in their calculating power, but also in how algorithms offer models for abstraction, engendering a multiplicity of solutions that can be explored for a wide range of problems. In projects such as RC11's project Equal Rights of Space (2021), AI plays a double role: it is both a disruptive social and economic condition that demands a radical reconfiguration of urban environments and a design instrument. The project imagines how future central business districts will evolve as a result of the replacement of intellectual tasks by AI. The final proposal envisions a future scenario for La Défense, in Paris, in which clusters of towers have been superseded by a more diffuse urban model which grants equal access to resources and infrastructure.

What would the urbanism of learning algorithms be like? What aspects of urban life can data give designers access to? Under the title of Machine-Thinking Urbanism, RC14 researches how machine-learning methods can widen the remit of design to include factors normally excluded in designing cities. Machine learning correlates diverse data providing a communication method for human and nonhuman actors. This results in a dynamic data ecology in which material, social and environmental factors as well as more elusive ones such as taste or cognitive attention acquire design agency. Mood-ulated Subtopia (2022) studied how surfaces in cities are perceived in order to imagine a type of urbanism based on ray casting, the computer graphic technique of constructing images by projecting virtual beams in three-dimensional space. By designing from the point of view of the individual agent in space, the project team constructed a dynamic space based on data on spatial cognition (colour, sound, time) rather than physical forms. The final proposal reimagined Canary Wharf in London to challenge monotonous and highly controlled public areas of the financial district by introducing a series of ephemeral, time-based interventions.

Ubiquitous computing also unveils a new post-anthropocentric reality in which the impact of artificial systems on the natural biosphere manifests itself at a variety of scales and through multiple actors. RC16's research, titled DeepGreen, responds to this new posthuman condition by focusing on bio-computation to explore different forms of intelligence and their potential to generate new urban environments. No longer confined to microprocessors, intelligences are urban and materialise through communication flows, interspecies interaction and material organisation. The design research reconceives cities' infrastructures as a means to rethink consumption patterns and convert waste and pollution into raw materials for new processes of production. RC16's project Eco-Rehab (2022) exploits the properties of biological materials such as mycelium to address the presence of heavy metals in the ground in post-industrial areas. The project concentrates on the often overlooked layers of informality in cities as a condition to exploit to both supplement existing public services and engage diverse systems (animal, microbiological or digital) to conjure up new urban infrastructures.

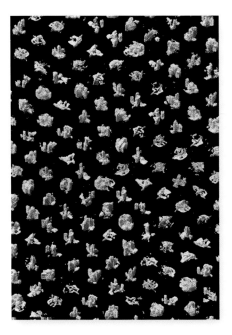

Wanting Ding, Peiwei Jiang, Yan Li, Di Wu and Fan Zhuang,
Equal Rights of Space,
B-Pro Urban Design RC11,
Bartlett School of Architecture,
University College London (UCL),
London,
2021

Equal Rights of Space imagined a new, decentralised La Défense – the iconic central business district of western Paris – based on an egalitarian system of spatial distribution. By combining social and urban data, machine-learning methods were deployed to reinvent the business district beyond the typology of the skyscraper. (RC11 is directed by Philippe Morel and Julian Besems.)

Qi Jiang, Hong Rong, Quan Zhou and Shaopo Huang,
Eco-Rehab,
B-Pro Urban Design RC16,
Bartlett School of Architecture,
University College London (UCL),
London,
2022

Based on the material properties of mycelia, Eco-Rehab speculates on the future spatial evolution of mycelium-human symbiosis through generative adversarial network (GAN) simulations. The new composite material remediates the soil by processing the heavy metals present in it and creates the conditions for a new urban habitat to emerge. (RC16 is directed by Claudia Pasquero and Filippo Nassetti.)

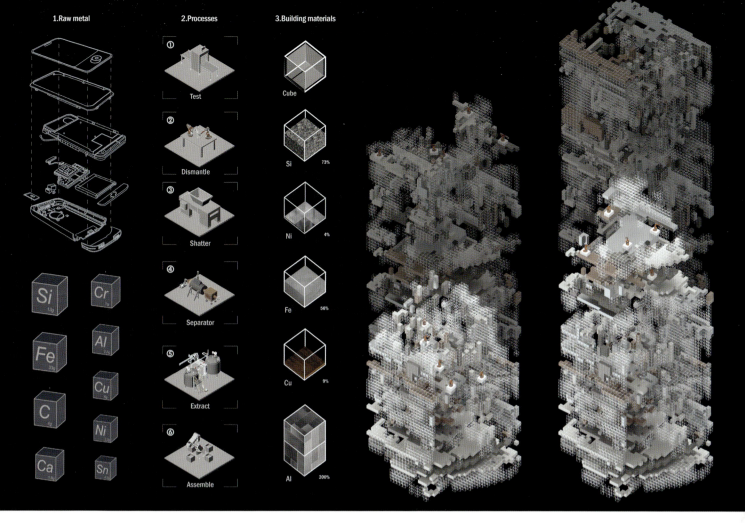

Posthumanism provides the conceptual instruments to charge design with ecological and political agendas. Under the title of Relational Urbanism, RC18 investigates 'planetary urbanisation' in which microscopic biochemical material cycles are entangled with large capital investments, giving rise to large global networks that shape the economy, culture and urbanism of cities. Such an approach calls for agile tactical design straddling between scales – to account for the nonlinearity of the Earth systems – and global stakeholders. RC18's Urban Mining project (2022) charts the networks governing the recycling of electronic waste in cities such as London to propose a new series of innovation hubs in which the discarded material can be repurposed. The project takes the form of a tower cropping up in London's skyline: an iconic gesture to signal the emergence of a different economy.

Ecological Intelligence
The building industry is historically slow in adopting disruptive innovation, instead opting for incremental improvements to its existing processes. The unprecedented nature of the challenges we face, coupled with rapid advancements in technology today, are shifting our perspective, giving way to new opportunities to change the very nature of our built environments at architectural, urban and territorial scales. We have the responsibility to adopt a posthuman vantage point so that human and nonhuman forms of intelligence not only co-exist but collaborate in shaping our environment. This shift in approach is not simply an incremental improvement, but a disruptive technological and cultural paradigm shift raising new questions surrounding how we design, build and co-inhabit our world. Through this lens the B-Pro challenges conventions of urban and architectural design, employing radical research-driven strategies that embed new forms of human and nonhuman agency in our built environment.

Xinjian Jiang, Guohui Liu and Man Zhang,
Urban Mining,
B-Pro Urban Design RC18,
Bartlett School of Architecture,
University College London (UCL),
London,
2022

Urban Mining proposes an urban prototype for the recycling of electronic waste. Added to existing buildings on UK high streets, old discarded phones enter the building and are transformed into valuable metal. The vertical stacking of the machinery to process e-waste gives an urban presence to the prototypes. (RC18 is directed by Enriqueta Llabres-Valls and Zachary Fluker.)

Notes
1. James Bridle, *Ways of Being: Beyond Human Intelligence*, Allen Lane (London), 2022.
2. See: https://www.ucl.ac.uk/bartlett/architecture/about-us/b-pro.

Text © 2024 John Wiley & Sons Ltd. Images © The Bartlett School of Architecture, University College London (UCL)

Ariane Lourie Harrison

FERAL SURFACES

BUILDING ENVELOPES AS INTELLIGENT MULTI-SPECIES HABITATS

Harrison Atelier,
Pollinators Pavilion,
Hudson,
New York,
2021

below: The surfaces of the Pollinators Pavilion – a visitors' centre and monitored native bee habitat designed and built by Harrison Atelier – demonstrate how building cladding can create habitats for other species.

opposite: The front of the Ductal concrete panel includes a rain-canopy protecting the entrance of nesting tubes for native bees. An endoscopic camera is located above the nesting tubes.

Designing architectural interventions for many species that function and are hospitable for a variety of occupants, creating convivial habitats at a range of scales, is a preoccupation of Brooklyn-based Harrison Atelier. Founder and principal **Ariane Lourie Harrison** leads us through some of the design collective's award-winning projects. As well as encouraging animal inhabitants, the firm's architecture is also smart, observing and recording activity to register data often not previously available.

The term 'feral' refers to animals that are wild or untamed, yet it derives from the Latin *feralis*, meaning funerary, or belonging to the dead. The deadly dimension of climate change is significant for nonhumans; environmental philosopher Timothy Morton suggests we replace the term 'climate change' with a term more concretely embedded in its effects: 'mass extinction'.[1] With the Anthropocene period comes evidence of Earth's sixth mass extinction: half of the planet's roughly two million identified species exist perilously, under threat of extinction due to human-caused habitat loss and environmental degradation.[2] This sixth mass extinction includes an 'insect apocalypse', the estimated loss of 75 per cent of insects over the past 50 years, undermining the very foundations of the terrestrial food webs.[3]

Feral tangles together the animal, wildness, funerary and the dead, to invoke the losses of habitat for most nonhuman species. 'Habitat' is a significant term for architecture as a discipline that designs such spaces for humans, but how does architecture address potential habitats for nonhuman species? Harrison Atelier designs surfaces that are habitats which envision coexistence yet integrate monitoring systems so as to contribute to scientific data gaps, arguing that the building as well as individuals can perform as 'citizen scientists'.

More-than-Posthuman
In designing surfaces that integrate insect, vegetal and machinic cavities, Harrison Atelier's work addresses the 'more-than-human' dimension of the posthuman.

The boundaries of this elastic term – 'posthuman' – have stretched since its articulation in the late 1970s by Ihab Hassan in the context of performance and technology.[4] By the first decades of the 21st century, the concept of posthuman architecture could be discerned in buildings that included Marco Casagrande's Ruin Academy in Taipei (2014), R&Sie(n)'s I'm Lost in Paris house in the French capital (2008) and The Living's Living Light in Seoul (2009).[5] If posthuman and post-Anthropocene discourses offered ways to question the anthropocentric bias of architecture, these terms continued to obscure the settler colonialism and constructions of race and gender that remained intact, by means of their relative invisibility, in the construction and conceptualisation of the relationships between human and nonhuman.

Zakiyyah Iman Jackson, Professor and Director of the Center for Feminist Research at the University of Southern California, demonstrates how the posthuman discourse glosses over systemic racism and animalisation of indigenous and Afro-descended humans in her book *Becoming Human: Matter and Meaning in an Antiblack World* (2020).[6] Drawing on Jamaican novelist Sylvia Wynter's significant body of decolonialist scholarship, professor and author Tiffany Lethabo King elaborates in a 2017 paper on the strategic omission of race constructions in Deleuzian posthumanist theory, which elide the racial politics that confer the very identity of human.[7] Bringing these issues into architecture and design, the

Harrison Atelier, *Feral Surfaces*,
MODEL Barcelona Architectures Festival,
Barcelona, Spain,
2023

left: The mycelium surface of the *Feral Surfaces* installation offers an example of monitored habitat for native bees. These panels were relocated to gardens in May 2023 following the MODEL Barcelona Architectures Festival for which they were commissioned.

Harrison Atelier, *Hempcrete Habitats*,
'Experimental Landings' exhibition,
Governors Island, New York,
2022

below: Hempcrete panels are proposed in this rendering as cladding for the base of the Manhattan Bridge, in addition to vermiculated stonework grilles to absorb stormwater.

anthology *More-than-Human* (2021), edited by architects Andrés Jaque, Marina Otero Verzier and curator Lucia Pietroiusti,[8] and the rich body of work by philosopher Rosi Braidotti, draw out the intersectional and transdisciplinary dimensions of the term 'posthuman'.[9] This recent scholarship connects critical race and gender theory to the teaching and practice of posthuman and more-than-human architecture in programmes that span from the living experiment of the Zoöp at Het Nieuwe Instituut in Rotterdam (2022) to the New European Bauhaus projects, which include the Garden Caretaker multi-species work (2023) guided by NXT's Madeleine Kate McGowan.[10]

In articulating a position for the architecture of nonhuman habitats, it is necessary to consider terms that move away from the armature of the human: terms such as 'multi-species design', for which designer and professor Daniel Metcalf offers a comprehensive genealogy as well as his own written and design work in this area.[11] Alternatively, the term 'feral' manifests an ecological awareness of the debilitated state of habitats today. Facing the monumentality of habitat loss equates to facing those without habitat. 'Posthuman' still sounds all too human.

NXT,
The Garden Caretaker,
Herlev,
Copenhagen, Denmark,
2023

opposite top: Among the New European Bauhaus projects, The Garden Caretaker explores multi-species community, place and urban ecologies through an inhabitation of an asphalt factory site in Herlev.

Holes and Habitats

Harrison Atelier's *Feral Surfaces* installation, a temporary mycelium-panelled landscape of native bee habitats, was commissioned for the 2023 MODEL Barcelona Architectures Festival organised through the Fundació Mies van der Rohe. Under the artistic direction of Eva Franch i Gilabert, the Festival examined how design can instigate new understandings between species, materials, classes and generations, effectively staging 'Radical Empathy' across a swathe of the city.[12] The tiny scales of insect existence rarely register with human concerns, to the degree that we can only estimate the dramatic loss of insect species, because only about 1 per cent of insects have been assessed.[13] And yet, insects are critical to the existence of most terrestrial species. *Feral Surfaces* assembles native plants and several thousand mycelium panels – each a native bee habitat – to enumerate, visualise and count these pollinators as denizens of the urban space.

Sited on a massive concrete plaza, the installation speaks to the difficulty of maintaining native bees' simple habitat – a hole in the ground – in our current urban, agricultural and industrial landscapes. Lack of habitat constitutes one of the major threats to all species, including for native bees, which constitute 90 per cent of the planet's 25,000 bee species, responsible for 75 per cent of non-agricultural pollination globally.[14] While these bees are diverse in size, colour and foraging – representing the biodiversity of each continent – the majority are considered 'solitary', that is, they do not form hives and social structures. Their inhabitation is for nesting (laying eggs and provisioning the future larvae) and tends to be opportunistic and discreet – in patches of bare earth, abandoned burrows and hollow reeds. Native bees lay three to six eggs in a nest, flying from nest to flower, working alone. Unlike honeybees that fly up to 12 kilometres (7.5 miles) for food, solitary bees forage no further than 50 metres (165 feet).[15] The *Feral Surfaces* installation takes this dimension – 50 metres per side – to visualise the restricted space between flower and nest for these bees, demonstrating the constraints on native bee habitats.

Harrison Atelier,
Feral Surfaces,
MODEL Barcelona Architectures Festival,
Barcelona, Spain,
2023

opposite bottom: Shown here in a drone view, the installation occupied a concrete parking garage with a constructed landscape that provided seating for 50 people and habitat for 2,000 solitary bees. Each side measured 50 metres (165 feet), the distance a native bee can fly between nest and floral resource.

left: The 2,500-square-metre (27,000-square-foot) installation contains 2,000 mycelium panels in addition to gardens with native bee-friendly plants.

The installation offers a landscape of native bee-friendly plants (lavender, salvia and other plants sourced from the Barcelona Biodiversity Atlas) and over 2,000 mycelium bee habitat panels. Each panel is about 6 centimetres (2.4 inches) thick; each contains a 10-centimetre (4-inch) diagonal tubular cavity drilled into it as a potential habitat for a cavity-dwelling solitary bee; each has a single hole about 1 centimetre (less than half an inch) in diameter as the entrance to the habitat. This type of simple habitat – a hole in the ground – is no longer easy to find, given human urbanisation and land development. The hole becomes a defining element of this habitat: it needs to be protected, framed and designed. The installation provokes an attention to building surfaces and cladding as an important potential locus for creating novel habitat.

While Harrison Atelier's written work has articulated the aesthetic dimensions of the hole, from sublime to eco-horror, built work dwells on more minute dimensions. Holes from 1 to 2 centimetres (⅜ to ¾ inch) accommodate the varied sizes of cavity-nesting inhabitants in many of the practice's projects. For example, the Pollinators Pavilion in Hudson, New York (2021) creates monitored or smart habitat for native pollinators on the exterior. Commissioned by Stone House Farms, whose 2,500 acres (1,000 hectares) for regenerative agriculture reflect the mission of the Rockefeller family's American Farmland Trust, the Pollinators Pavilion serves as a visitor centre as well as a demonstration space for novel native bee habitat. The domed structure is clad in hundreds of concrete panels which provide over 1,500 nesting tubes for solitary bees. The panels feature protruding canopies, sheltering the bees' nesting tubes from rain. Panels also make space for monitoring systems comprising endoscopic cameras and microprocessors. The artificial habitat is able to produce photographs of the nesting bees in addition to sheltering them.

Monitoring becomes a critical part of the artificial habitat, given the aforementioned fact that only 1 per cent of insects' conservation status has been assessed and that there remain large gaps in scientific data on solitary bees. Harrison Atelier works with entomologists and integrates artificial-intelligence (AI) models to automate insect identification of the pollinators by harvesting millions of images from on-site cameras, and continuing to train an AI model for identification at the family (not species) level.[16] Research on the potential of AI for insect identification describes the need for 'effective continuous and noninvasive observation'.[17] Harrison Atelier's work suggests that effective and noninvasive observation of insect life, along with the creation of novel habitats, can also be achieved by the surfaces of buildings, were these designed for more than human use.

The French philosopher Jacques Rancière's *The Politics of Aesthetics: The Distribution of the Sensible* offers the insight that the political appears when those who are not officially counted make themselves heard and seen.[18] Politics involves becoming seen and becoming counted among planetary entities. Consider the 2,000 holes in the *Feral Surfaces* installation, along with the 1,500 cavities of the Pollinators Pavilion, as attempts to propose an architectural surface that counts every solitary bee among urban denizens and brings them into our ethical regard.

```
Sara Mountford,
Snail Habitat,
MArch,
Yale School of Architecture,
2023
```

This proposal by student Sara Mountford was developed in Ariane Harrison's 'Feral Systems' seminar and envisages a habitat for land snails and native slugs on the glazing of Diller Scofidio + Renfro's Columbia Business School in New York (2022).

Feral Systems

The feral has occupied our cities throughout the history of architecture, from Piranesi's 'Views of Rome' in the 18th century to the imaginary of Gotham city in the 20th; from coyotes curled up in empty buses to eagles with Instagram accounts following their ledge-lifestyle. That the city already provides a proxy to a wilderness merits closer attention.

Cities are increasingly understood to represent critical biodiversity preserves: Singapore and Berlin set examples for their documentation of urban biodiversity, while the European Green Deal emphasises efforts to promote habitats for nonhumans in cities.[19] As human population increases and the planet urbanises, habitat for other species will continue to disappear if our cities do not become sites of resilience. The surfaces of buildings offer both the image and function of resilience in providing habitat.

In contrast to reflective corporate towers or glazed residential complexes, the textured materials of 'premodern' structures provided a literal living space for nonhumans. Working today in more ecologically conscious materials would contribute new palettes of texture to house nonhumans on building surfaces, allowing the façade to demonstrate a more inclusive address of planetary life, as prototypes by a few firms – including New York-based Terreform ONE and COOKFOX as well as Harrison Atelier – suggest. Neither smooth nor monolithic, a feral envelope invokes the qualities of wildness, overgrowth, decay and metabolic cycling of elements that attends organic processes.

Could urban façades integrate feral systems to provide habitat for multiple species, and in so doing, create new perspectives for the urban dweller? A feral system as a strategy for adaptive reuse of buildings represents one avenue for developing urban biodiversity. Feral systems allow us to manifest a collaborative effort between humans, animals and machines while remaining keenly aware of the tenuous existence of all species on a warming planet. ᴅ

Notes

1. Timothy Morton, *Being Ecological*, MIT Press (Cambridge, MA), 2018, p 36.
2. International Union for Conservation of Nature and Natural Resources (IUCN) Red List: https://www.iucnredlist.org/resources/summary-statistics.
3. Brooke Jarvis, 'The Insect Apocalypse is Here', *The New York Times Magazine*, 27 November 2018, p 41: https://www.nytimes.com/2018/11/27/magazine/insect-apocalypse.html.
4. Ihab Hassan, 'Prometheus as Performer: Toward a Posthuman Culture?', *Georgia Review* 31, 1977, pp 830–50.
5. All case studies in Ariane Lourie Harrison (ed), *Architectural Theories of the Environment: Posthuman Territory*, Routledge (New York), 2013.
6. Zakiyyah Iman Jackson, *Becoming Human: Matter and Meaning in an Antiblack World*, New York University Press (New York), 2020.
7. Tiffany Lethabo King, 'Humans Involved: Lurking in the Lines of Posthumanist Flight', *Critical Ethnic Studies* 3 (1), Spring 2017, pp 162–85; Sylvia Wynter, 'No Humans Involved', *Forum NHI Knowledge for the 21st Century* 1 (1), 1994, pp 42–73.
8. Andrés Jaque, Marina Otero Verzier and Lucia Pietroiusti (eds), *More-than-Human*, Het Nieuwe Instituut (Rotterdam), 2021.
9. Rosi Braidotti, *Posthuman Knowledge*, Polity Press (Cambridge and Medford, MA), 2019.
10. See 'Multi-species Community, Explorations of Place, and Urban Landscapes', Haveværtens programme, New European Bauhaus: https://www.nxtbrand.dk/blog/open-call-for-artists-the-garden-caretaker/.
11. Daniel J Metcalfe, *Multispecies Design*, unpublished PhD thesis, University of the Arts London, 2015.
12. MODEL Barcelona Architecture Festival 2023: https://www.model.barcelona/edicio2023/en.
13. Julia Janicki *et al*, 'The Collapse of Insects', Reuters, 6 December 2022: https://www.reuters.com/graphics/GLOBAL-ENVIRONMENT/INSECT-APOCALYPSE/egpbykdxjvq/.
14. USGS Communications on native bees, 15 June 2015: https://www.usgs.gov/news/featured-story/buzz-native-bees.
15. Antonia Zurbuchen *et al*, 'Maximum Foraging Ranges in Solitary Bees: Only Few Individuals Have the Capability to Cover Long Foraging Distances', *Biological Conservation* 143 (3), 2010, pp 669–76.
16. Microsoft AI for Earth grantee: https://microsoft.github.io/AIforEarth-Grantees/.
17. Toke T Høye *et al*, 'Deep Learning and Computer Vision Will Transform Entomology', *Proceedings of the National Academy of Sciences (PNAS)* 118 (2), 11 January 2021, pp 1–10: https://doi.org/10.1073/pnas.2002545117.
18. Jacques Rancière, *The Politics of Aesthetics: The Distribution of the Sensible*, tr Gabriel Rockhill, Continuum (London), 2004.
19. Fran Silverman, 'Cities Can Be Part of the Solution in Sustaining Species', *YSE Newsletter*, 28 February 2022: https://environment.yale.edu/news/article/cities-can-be-part-solution-sustaining-species.

Text © 2024 John Wiley & Sons Ltd. Images: pp 38–41, 42(b), 43 © Harrison Atelier; p 42(t) © Madeleine Kate McGowan; pp 44–5 © Sara Mountford

Mario Carpo

On the Posthuman Charm of Slime and Mould

ecoLogicStudio (Claudia Pasquero and Marco Poletto)
with the Urban Morphogenesis Lab at the Bartlett School
of Architecture, University College London, and the
Synthetic Landscape Lab at the University of Innsbruck,
in collaboration with the United
Nations Development Program,
DeepGreen Guatemala City,
2020

Redesign of the municipal waste collection networks of Guatemala City using a generative adversorial network (GAN) algorithm trained on the behaviour of a *Physarum polycephalum* slime mould.

Slime moulds have no central nervous system and are single-cell organisms, yet they can build communities of themselves to create complex, food-foraging cooperative networks. They are even known to solve mazes in search of something to eat. **Mario Carpo**, Reyner Banham Professor of Architectural History and Theory at the Bartlett School of Architecture, University College London, explains the unique position of slime moulds in recent complexity and emergence studies.

It would take a great philosopher, and historian, to explain the reasons of the popularity of slime moulds among postmodern thinkers, computational designers and political scientists of our time. And I would not even need to refer in this context to the figural proximity between slime moulds and the architectural blobs that have been a trope of digitally intelligent design since the mid-1990s. For I am not talking about visual metaphors here; I am talking of the real thing: free-living, single-cell entities (seen in the past as fungi) which, at some point in their life cycle look like gelatinous, semi-liquid, vaguely animated substances that appear to emanate from, and trickle upon, rotten or decomposing organic matter.

Slime moulds were the protagonist of Steven Johnson's 2001 best-selling *Emergence: The Connected Lives of Ants, Brains, Cities, and Software*, a book that powerfully contributed to the popularisation of complexity theory among the general public. Slime moulds have long intrigued scientists due to their capacity to alternate from monocellular life to multicellular aggregates, and back, depending on environmental conditions; in the late 1960s studies by philosopher, physicist and feminist Evelyn Fox Keller, and by mathematician Lee Segel, suggested that the shift in the life patterns of slime moulds occurs due to spontaneous, local reactions, in the absence of any coordinated communication among the colony of cells, and slime moulds have been widely seen since then as a case-study of biological self-organisation.

Self-organisation is in turn a staple of complexity science, which (starting with Warren Weaver's pioneering studies from 1947–58) deals with phenomena that emerge from the interaction of individual 'agents' following rules of behaviour determined solely by mutual proximity – a definition which almost coincides with that of cellular automata, a new kind of maths derived from studies carried out by John von Neumann and Stanisław Ulam at the Los Alamos National Laboratory from 1947 to the late 1950s, apparently independently from Weaver's then inchoate theories of complexity. In his 2001 book, Johnson goes on to recount Mitchel Resnick's experiments with computer renderings of slime mould aggregations, and Resnick's design of StarLogo, a slime-mould-inspired, agent-based computer program meant to simulate and visualise the behaviour of self-organising systems for educational purposes. StarLogo is described in Resnick's 1994 book *Turtles, Termites, and Traffic Jams*, where Resnick also gives an account of Marvin Minsky's reservations and objections. Resnick claims that eventually even Minsky became a slime-mould fan. Be that as it may, Steven Johnson was evidently a believer. As he stated: 'When I imagine the shape that will hover above the first half of the 21st century, what comes to mind is […] the pulsing red and green pixels of Mitch Resnick's slime mould simulations, moving erratically across the screen at first, then slowly coalescing into later forms. […] I see them on the screen, growing and dividing, and I think: That way lies the future.'[1]

Architecture, Complexity and Moulds

Architecture was a very early stakeholder in the shaping of the postmodern (or rather anti-modern) theory of complexity. Jane Jacobs, whose seminal *The Death and Life of Great American Cities* (1961)[2] is unanimously seen today as a keystone of 20th-century urban theory, was familiar with the 1958 Rockefeller Foundation Annual Report, where Warren Weaver had summarised his theory of 'organized complexity'. Jacobs cited Weaver extensively, and terms and notions of Weaver's theory of complexity contributed to her idea of cities. Jacobs's point was that cities are made of people, not of buildings, and should be made by people, not by planners (today we would call that a bottom-up approach to urbanism), but since Jacobs's infusion of elements of complexity theory into urban studies, cities have often been seen and studied as independent, organic phenomena capable of creative self-organisation; in more recent times this has incited designers and planners to model cities and city life using cellular automata – and even slime moulds, both real and simulated.

For all that, and regardless of Robert Venturi's 1966 famed but mostly anecdotal foray into the language (not the theory) of complexity theory, complexity science remained mostly foreign to design culture and architectural theory until the surge of computer-aided design and the rise of digital design theory in the early 1990s. In the late 1990s designers would have been familiar with some threads and strands of complexity

Frequency chart produced in Google Books Ngram Viewer, 2023

Chart of frequencies of the combined occurrence of the terms 'slime mould' and 'architecture' in books published in English from 1950 to 2019.

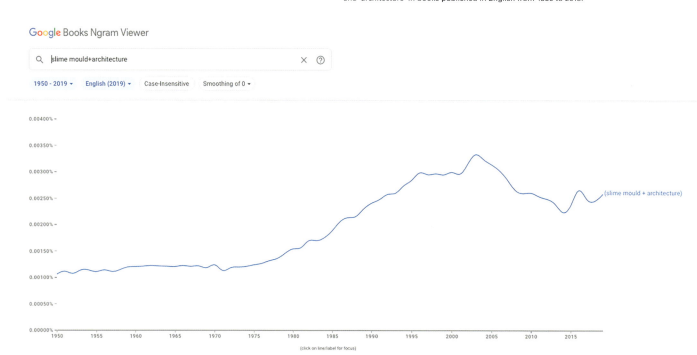

science through the writings of Sanford Kwinter, Manuel DeLanda and Kevin Kelly, among others; Charles Jencks's capital but often misunderstood *The Architecture of the Jumping Universe* (1995) offered the first systematic primer of complexity theory for the use of the design professions.[3] But it is at the Emergent Technologies and Design (EmTech) Master Programme at the Architectural Association School of Architecture (AA) in London in the first decade of the new century that a creative conflation of complexism, computationalism and architectural theory was successfully transmuted into a conceptual framework that was both relevant and hugely appealing to cutting-edge computational design research; and the idea of emergence that was forged at the AA during those years soon spread to the computational design community around the world, and it remains to this day (2024) one of the most pervasive and influential design theories of our time, and one that has already left an indelible trace on design history and on the history of architectural education around the world. The Emergence and Design Group was founded in 2001 by Michael Weinstock, Michael Hensel and Achim Menges, and the group guest-edited several issues of △, of which the first, *Emergence: Morphogenetic Design Strategies*, published in 2004, is reportedly the best-selling △ issue ever.[4]

Yet by that time a different feature of slime moulds was retaining the attention of scientists – and computer scientists in particular. Studies by Japanese biologist Toshiyuki Nakagaki published around the year 2000 (and briefly mentioned by Johnson[5]) demonstrated that slime moulds have mysterious but remarkably effective ways of finding the shortest way inside a labyrinth when looking for food, thus suggesting that they must have computational capacities – never mind that slime moulds, being monocellular beings without any embryological differentiation, do not even have a nervous system, let alone a brain. Scientists now believe that slime moulds can solve mazes by leaving biological traces or markers on dead-end itineraries they tried and retracted from, so they can exclude them from further searches. Slime moulds' problem-solving skills would hence appear to be based on some kind of trial-and-error process, and their capacity to learn from random mistakes can be seen as a primitive decision-making strategy – of the kind that early computer scientists developed into iterative processes known to this day as 'hill-climbing' or gradient-based optimisation.

Slimy Computation

Computer scientists were even more puzzled when it also appeared that the gelatinous bodies of slime moulds can at times approximate a peculiar family of smooth curves used by engineers to optimise aerodynamic streamlining, or by financial analysts to interpolate between points in a graph (Bézier curves, splines, etc), thus lending weight to the idea that the very unintelligent slime moulds should in fact be seen as extremely efficient biological computers. Slime moulds are somewhat slower in their daily operations than silicon chips, so the practical applications of this discovery

Andrew Adamatzky, 'Slime Mould Gates, Roads and Sensors', 2015

below: Computer scientist Adamatzky's *Atlas of Physarum Computing* (World Scientific (Hackensack, NJ), 2015) explores the intelligent spatial activity of the slime mould *Physarum polycephalum*, as shown here through illustrations from its first chapter. In this image, a *Physarum* slime mould foraging a topography of the Balkans where food has been placed in the locations of major settlements in the Roman age recreates the historical layout of Roman roads.

bottom: This slime mould, foraging on a three-dimensional nylon model of the USA, imitates migratory itineraries between Mexico and the US. Migratory links developed on a flat substrate may represent air transportation while routes on three-dimensional terrain signify ground transportation.

are likely to be modest; but the epistemological and even philosophical implications are not. For, if we have a look at the bigger picture, we must come to the almost inevitable conclusion that the most advanced operations of today's machine learning (based on iterative computational trial and error and subsequent 'survival of the fittest' optimisation of results) is very similar to the problem-solving processes of the less intelligent beings on Earth. Furthermore, both problem-solving strategies – those of artificial intelligence (AI), and those of slime moulds – appear to be equally at odds with the problem-solving strategy of natural (ie organic) human intelligence, which derives from, and builds upon, comparison, selection, generalisation, formalisation and abstraction – in short, on our capacity to construe intelligible general statements that go beyond our recorded experience. This, it seems, is what neither posthuman computers nor infra-human, or pre-human, slime moulds can do.

For the sake of clarity, it must be stated that the two skills for which slime moulds are celebrated today as unlikely but reliable scientific models (of emergent self-organisation, and of computational machine learning, respectively) pertain in fact to two different species of slime moulds: the self-organising slime mould that assembles into a cluster acting as a single multi-cellular entity is a 'cellular' slime mould (those described by Johnson are of the *Dictyostelium* genus); whereas the computational slime mould that solves mazes and draws splines is a 'plasmodial' slime mould (that favoured by contemporary designers and engineers is of a species called *Physarum polycephalum*). The two scientific models also have very different philosophical allegiances: emergence and self-organisation relate to a view of nature that is often party to an ideological view of the world – one which is shared by today's libertarians and by many of the most unsavoury right-wing ideologies of our time. A complexist scientist today would convincingly

ecoLogicStudio (Claudia Pasquero
and Marco Poletto) with the
Urban Morphogenesis Lab at the
Bartlett School of Architecture,
University College London, and the
Synthetic Landscape Lab
at the University of Innsbruck,
in collaboration with the United
Nations Development Program,
DeepGreen Guatemala City,
2020

opposite top: Diagram of the design process.

Andrew Adamatzky,
'Slime Mould Gates,
Roads and Sensors',
2015

left: Laid on an isotropic nutrient substrate, a *Physarum polycephalum* slime mould expands as an omnidirectional wave, partly isomorphic to the structure of an expanding galaxy.

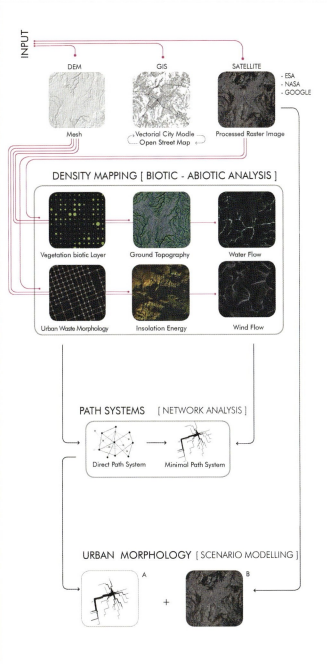

argue that the best way to regulate traffic in a metropolis is to eliminate all traffic regulations (and would provide proof thereof, as Per Bak did in 1996[6]); extrapolating from the same argument, but without the benefit of proof, a true believer in complexism and self-organisation today would conclude that the best city planning consists in the abolition of all planning, and the most efficient social organisation of all times is the jungle, where natural selection, or 'survival of the fittest' optimisation, has served Nature well since the beginning of time.

Computational problem-solving by heuristic programming and core search, by contrast, is just a technology – one we have adopted because it works, and one which has served computer science well since its inception around 1956. Yet the common reference of machine learning, and of complexity science, to the archetypal slime mould is a useful reminder of how much the posthuman, the pre-human and the bestial have in common. Slime moulds, Nature in general and AI alike do not design, and neither do they plan. That alone would appear to make them all equally uneasy bedfellows for the design and planning professions, but so it goes. Slime moulds just react to things that happen around them, and they survive by merging with similar cells when food is scarce, or by avoiding dead-ends when foraging for food. Nature has had plenty of time to carry out an unimaginable number of equally blind and random trials, and Nature as we see it around us shows some of the very few that happened not to be errors. Computers do not have so much time to keep trying, but they are much faster than Nature, which is why trial and error is a viable AI problem-solving strategy and, for a certain range of problem, either the best or the only available. Humans, however, can learn both by experience and by schooling; there are languages we learn by imitating the first words we hear as children and languages we learn by memorising the rules of grammar from books. Slime moulds do not have that choice. In the 1970s and 1980s we did try to train computers by putting all the rules in the world into their memory, and it famously didn't work – now we know that machine learning works much better. But humans that choose to learn by trial and error when the transmission of accumulated knowledge is otherwise available are neither pre-human nor posthuman; they are wasteful fools. ⌂

Slime moulds, Nature in general and AI alike do not design, and neither do they plan. That alone would appear to make them all equally uneasy bedfellows for the design and planning professions

Notes
1. Steven Johnson, *Emergence: The Connected Lives of Ants, Brains, Cities, and Software*, Scribner (New York), 2001; citation is to the 2012 reprint, p 23.
2. Jane Jacobs, *The Death and Life of Great American Cities*, Random House (New York), 1961.
3. Charles Jencks, *The Architecture of the Jumping Universe: A Polemic*, Academy Editions (London), 1995.
4. Michael Hensel, Achim Menges and Michael Weinstock (eds), ⌂ *Emergence: Morphogenetic Design Strategies*, May/June (no 3), 2004. See Mario Carpo, *Beyond Digital: Design and Automation at the End of Modernity*, MIT Press (Cambridge, MA), 2023, pp 106–9; and Christina Cogdell, *Towards a Living Architecture? Complexism and Biology in Generative Design*, University of Minnesota Press (Minneapolis, MN), 2018, pp 28–30, 35–8.
5. Johnson, *op cit*.
6. Per Bak, *How Nature Works: The Science of Self-Organized Criticality*, Springer (New York), 1996, pp 183–98.

Text © 2024 John Wiley & Sons Ltd. Images: pp 46–7, 51 © ecoLogicStudio; pp 49–50 © Andrew Adamatzky

**Colbey Reid and
Dennis Weiss**

alternative domiciles for the domestic posthuman

Certain Measures (Tobias Nolte, Andrew Witt,
Olivia Heung and Valentin Zellmer),
Home Is Where the Droids Are,
Housing the Human Festival,
Radial System,
Berlin,
2019

The designers describe their installation as a playful exploration of an imagined future in which robots, not humans, are the primary occupants of houses. It investigates the combination of utility, ornament and companionship provided by robots in a world where robots, pets, plants and objects are all treated as equal stakeholders in a home. This enables the architects to imagine future homes as menageries that can congregate wherever all their parts gather, rendering mobility the pre-eminent component of smart domesticity.

What are the most appropriate domestic notions, designs and surroundings for posthumans to flourish throughout the different phases of their life? **Colbey Reid**, Professor and Chair of Fashion Studies at Columbia College Chicago, and **Dennis Weiss**, Professor of Philosophy at York College of Pennsylvania, explore these terrains and posit some speculative futures that steer away from the sterile Modernist minimalism often portrayed as the contemporary aesthetics of the smart home, towards a more diverse, expressive and expansive collective of visual and haptic interfaces and social interactions – between posthumans, their contextual machinic ecologies and their communities.

Where does a posthuman live? Posthumans are typically portrayed as emerging fully formed from the minds of scientists and engineers within institutional settings such as labs, hospitals, offices and governments. These environments are perhaps more aptly conceived of as containers for posthumans rather than what one might traditionally call a home. Moreover, what posthumans do within their places of containment falls short of the conventional notion of living, since while the term 'living' can refer to simply being alive, it also carries significant connotations of home-centred lifestyles, enacted through a particular design register. *Hospital Living* and *Lab Living* are not magazines whose pages anyone would pore over, not even emerging posthuman species. While being considered alive in contemporary times might involve elements of technoscience, the concept of living still resonates strongly as a decorative art form.

Competing Imaginative Visions

Designing the posthuman home has nevertheless been a longstanding preoccupation within the realm of speculative futures. The notion of 'smart homes' has given rise to various models. Consider two from the early 1960s: Disney's Carousel of Progress in Florida, and the Rogers family household in *The Twilight Zone* episode 'I Sing the Body Electric'.[1] These examples offer contrasting perspectives on what it means to embody 'smartness' within a home environment. In the case of the Carousel of Progress, a sense of optimism infuses the portrayal of technological wonders integrated into the home, focused on convenience, functionality, efficiency and progress. The technology primarily consists of appliances that enable a traditional (white, Western, nuclear) family to navigate their world with comfort and ease. While the idea that technology might eventually supplant humans had yet to be conceived in the 1960s, it is notable that the human family depicted already assumes a subservient role; the humans serve as demonstrators of the technology's capabilities, becoming instruments of the technology they coexist with.

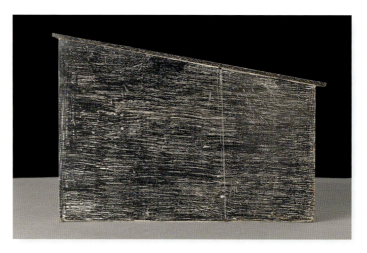

Ross Sawyers,
The Future Isn't What it Used To Be,
2023

The Chicago photographer Ross Sawyers's imaginary houses explore dystopian and utopian depictions of homes without human presence or interior design. Modelled on real-world homes throughout history, from prehistoric cave dwellings to spindled skyscrapers, each alternative architectural style conjures the sense of longing for different kinds of human living and alternatively forged human communities.

Bohlin Cywinski Jackson and Cutler Anderson Architects,
Xanadu 2.0,
Medina, Washington,
1988

Bill Gates may own the quintessential example of what most of us imagine when we think of a modern smart home: one packed with enough technology to give the owner the sense of living in a video game. However, little thought is given in conventional smart home design to the elements most of us associate with the 'homeyness' of home life. Do these homey components contradict or comprise the smartness we refer to when we talk about smart home design?

Folayemi Wilson,
Eliza's Peculiar Cabinet of Curiosities,
Lynden Sculpture Garden,
Milwaukee, Wisconsin,
2016

Folayemi Wilson's ongoing Afrofuturist installation is a full-scale reproduction of a 19th-century slave cabin, home to a fictional woman of African descent named Eliza. Eliza's 'smart home' is comprised of its cabinet-like quality for assembling myriad collectible objects through which Eliza is networked to other people across various spaces and time in the natural and built environment.

In contrast, the episode of *The Twilight Zone* presents a person at the heart of the smart home: 'an electronic data processing system in the shape of an elderly woman' who has 'the incredible ability of giving loving supervision to your family'.[2] Anticipating the 21st-century emergence of Japanese eldercare robots like the Robear, this portrayal shifts the idea of smartness away from efficient progress and instead emphasises caregiving and companionship; an android grandmother fills the emotional needs of a grieving family – itself non-traditional and diverse in its inclusion of a non-biological relative – by forming emotional bonds with them. The technology's chief function is to support the family's navigation through difficult and complex emotional situations. Unlike the sleek surface-level efficiency of the previous vision, this home's smartness lies in its capacity to engage deeply with the complexities inherent in the human experience.

Designing for Domestic Posthumans
Our proposed framework for domestic posthuman design aims to shift posthumans out of the impersonal digital networks and sterile technoscientific domains they have hitherto inhabited, into the more familiar and humanising habitat of the home.[3] It is within homes, not labs and computer networks, that human persons are nurtured in their early years of life. These spaces facilitate acts of care and experiences of connection with both human and

nonhuman others. They help integrate new humans into the lives and bodies of caregivers, neighbours, friends and pets, and an array of domestic elements such as furniture, toys, clothes, blankets and food. Posthumans are likely to not only need, but will also emerge from the complex networks of persons and objects that we nurture and are nurtured by in our homes.

Deriving from the application of a feminist, care-oriented philosophical framework to posthumanism, the concept of the domestic posthuman reminds us that humans do not spring into existence as 22- to 65-year-old adults. Instead, human experience comprises various stages from infancy to old age, and encompasses a wide spectrum of needs and individuals with diverse abilities. These multivariate human entities are ushered through a series of developmental transitions under the collaborative guidance of family, or extended or chosen family, and using a range of parenting and caretaking techniques. The domestic posthuman person is thus always also a posthuman second person, brought into being through embodied, social and relational connections with others and objects. Designing for domestic posthuman second persons involves seeking creative ways of fostering connections, providing care and participating in the mending process. It requires exploring the neglected intersection between the posthuman and the home and homelike places, including gardens, play spaces and third places.

This brings us back to a slightly altered version of the initial question: in what kind of home does a domestic posthuman grow up, get taken care of, care for others, love and grow old? Conventional posthumanism promotes the smart home as the abode of advanced human evolutionary potential. Smart homes are typically defined by their digital connectivity and integration into the Internet of Things; they are a fusion of information networks and virtual media, hybrids of silicon, algorithms and flesh. However, a smart home's human-technology assemblages are often made of terms that remain insufficiently explored, referring only to small subsets of humans, technomaterialities and technofunctions. The aesthetic of smart homes typically embodies a sleek and minimalist modernism: flat surfaces, hard materials, angular. Traces of the inhabitants are concealed; everything is new and clean; and ornament and decoration are considered superfluous, undignified, indicative of pathology (hoarding) or materialism (overconsumption).

In contrast, the notion of a domestic posthuman emphasises a different design aesthetic that questions the current design discourses that reject decoration. Instead, it argues for the centrality of ornament in the context of the domestic posthuman experience. Living, in the sense of having a lifestyle, absolutely matters to the creation and cultivation of the domestic posthuman. It is vital to reposition interior and furniture design, alongside the acts of nesting, mending, puttering, loitering and acquisitive collecting, as pivotal elements in the creation of a domestic posthuman home. In essence, the goal is to reposition homemaking at the centre of house making.

BETA, 3 Generation House, Amsterdam, 2018

The house, consisting of two separate apartments joined by a central staircase, imagines multigenerational housing as a new paradigm of smart design which fosters cross-generational care. As designer Auguste van Oppen notes, 'It's about being there for one another.'

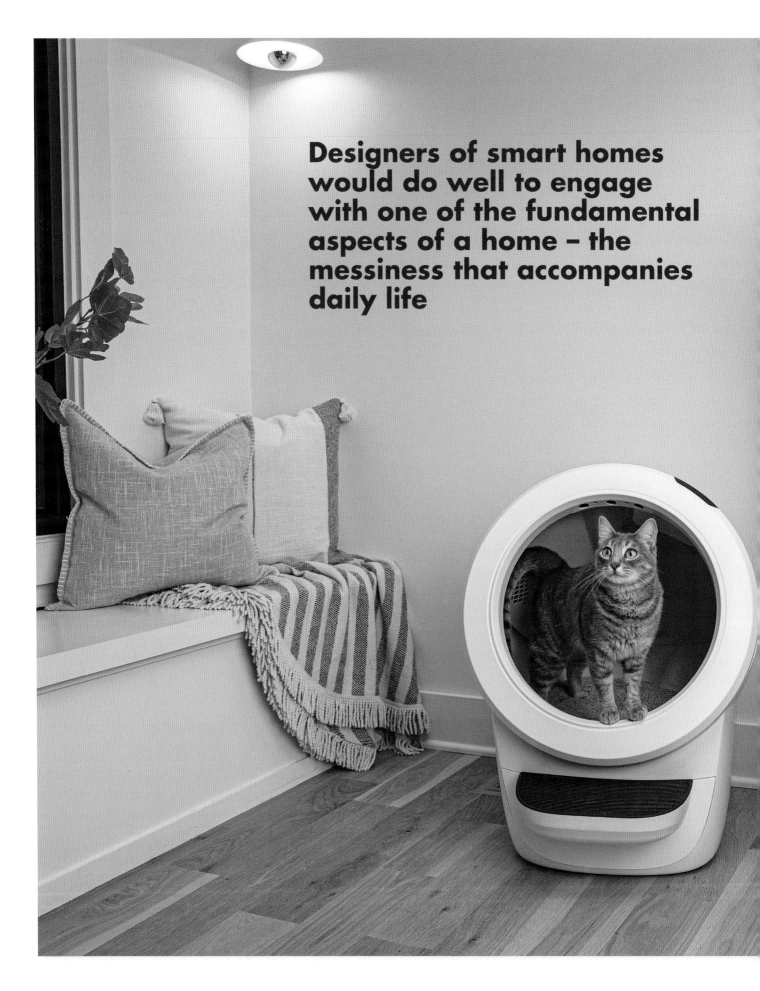

Designers of smart homes would do well to engage with one of the fundamental aspects of a home – the messiness that accompanies daily life

Whisker,
Litter-Robot 4,
2023

The automated smart home is often portrayed as a technological solution to life's messiness. Whisker's litter robot promises to make cat-life easier by removing the worst part: cleaning the litter box. But tending to the messiness of pet waste can be an act of care that affirms the shared animality of human beings and the nonhuman animals sharing their domestic spaces.

On Toilets, Televisions and Kitchens

In designing for domestic posthumans, we need to relinquish the fantasy of sterility and instead engage with human waste. In western smart home design, little attention is paid to toilet options, or to their underlying waste disposal systems. At best, smart homes may offer the luxury of Japanese-style toilets equipped with water jets and heaters – a variation of the conventional sewage system toilets prevalent in the Western world. Unfortunately, these systems contribute to a range of environmental crises, including algal blooms in bodies of water to which sewage is diverted, and soil depletion due to over-farming without sufficient re-fertilisation. Composting toilets, coupled with biogas systems, offer viable alternatives; they have gained significant popularity in contemporary China, creating a 'biogas boom' there. However, they remain conspicuously absent from the conversation in Western or Western-influenced architectural planning. This oversight extends to the consideration of organic and inorganic waste generated from food scraps, discarded items and packaging materials. Designers of smart homes would do well to engage with one of the fundamental aspects of a home – the messiness that accompanies daily life – and think deeply about the unglamorous, yet inherently human necessities of waste production and management. Exploring ancient and non-Western human waste disposal systems and toilet designs for inspiration might provide valuable insights with which to begin.

Screen management might be considered of secondary importance, yet its urgency is equally pronounced, indicating how a focus solely on efficient, convenient and hyperfunctional technology might not wholly address the needs of human existence. Consider the example of the television – once a fixture of the living room, then finding its way into bedrooms and kitchens, and now a device we carry with us. As screens gained mobility and personalisation, they transformed our viewing experience by disembodying and displacing it. The smart television screen has fostered a posthuman experience that echoes the individualism characteristic of neoliberalism. Netflix, for instance, provides separate avatars for each household member, served by algorithms curating tailored content for private consumption on individual laptops, tablets or smart TVs. Could we envision an alternate televisual experience that encourages conviviality, one that fosters connections not solely between algorithms, screens and individuals (forming a posthuman assemblage) but among a diverse community of others (comprising a domestic posthuman assemblage)?

Such a broader and more diverse network could encompass technomaterial and embodied relations. Such a vision might not be merely speculative. Remember when televisions were themselves furniture, bulky cathode-ray tubes concealed behind oak veneers and adorned with faux drawer knobs and pulls? What are the merits of embedding screens within furniture? For one, such ensembles inherently promote sociability – many people utilise them, often simultaneously, in ways reminiscent of shared experiences once common in public spaces and, until recently, integral to home life. It is worth advocating for a vision of the smart home that interfaces with furniture design, disarticulating core technologies of our era from digital and virtual domains and rearticulating them as tangible furniture.

There is also inspiration to be drawn from Genevieve Bell and Joseph Kaye's 'kitchen manifesto' (2002) in which they argue that 'to create spaces and technologies that people will want to use, not just admire from a distance, the domestic must be disentangled from the digital'.[4] Bell, a cultural anthropologist, and Kaye, a research scientist in human-computer interaction, contend that the smart-home movement over the past decade has progressed with scant consideration for users and occupants. As they note, 'In creating technology for the home, in particular for the kitchen, technologists have forgotten that these domestic spaces are inhabited and used by people.'[5] Consider Andrew Witt's proposition in 'Feral Autonomies' to dematerialise kitchens and living rooms by reformulating these places as domotic services. Witt, co-founder of the design office Certain Measures and Associate Professor of Practice in Architecture at the Harvard Graduate School of Design, envisions a feral domestic space in which technology embraces its animal instincts and homes are 'unbundled into autonomous technological services'.[6] In Certain Measures' Autonomous Home, the kitchen ceases to be the heart of the home, for the home has been

Stefano Boeri Architetti,
Wonderwoods Vertical Forest,
Utrecht, The Netherlands,
2023

Challenging the dichotomy between urban city and arboreal jungle, Stefano Boeri Architetti is building vertical forests in cities such as Milan, Utrecht, Dubai and Huanggang. These vertical forests include more than 300 trees that serve to integrate architecture and living nature, transforming vegetation from an ornamental element into an essential element of each project. They suggest a luscious and living posthuman home, entangling human beings, nature and the built environment into a smart assemblage to redefine urban living in an age of climate change.

dematerialised in favour of 'a choreography of services and furniture orbiting the occupant'.[7] The notion of the domestic posthuman seeks to challenge conventional cultural perceptions of current utilisation and potential approaches for the use of networked information technology within the home. It echoes Bell and Kaye's proposal about viewing spaces like the kitchen 'not just as a collection of wires, appliances, and Internet points, but as a space in which people really live'.[8] Thinking both domestically and digitally, Bell and Kaye propose a set of design guidelines that are not driven exclusively by technology; they incorporate attention to humans and their experiences (rule #4) and finding and supporting domestic rituals (rule #5).

Returning to the rephrased original question, 'In what kind of home does a domestic posthuman grow up, get taken care of, care for others, love and grow old?', one might ponder the prospects for children, the elderly and the disabled within a home transformed into services. Are human animals able to thrive in a cyber-zoo? The domestic posthuman does not reject technology, but digital technology is not its sole driving force while exploring the new facets of human experience brought about by our integration and assimilation with technology. Rather, designing for domestic posthumans begins with considerations of technologies conducive to care and conviviality, such as specific types of toilets, televisions and kitchens. The Rogers family's vision of a smart home does not dismiss technology. Sometimes, to manage a chaotic, dysfunctional family afflicted by loss, perhaps what is needed is an electronic-data-processing grandma. Most contemporary architectural visions of posthuman smart homes are not grandma-centric, or even grandma-aware. But perhaps they should be. It is possible that being so would make them smarter. ∆

Notes
1. *The Twilight Zone*, Season 3, Episode 35, 'I Sing the Body Electric', 1962. Directed by James Sheldon and William Claxton. Aired 18 May 1962 on CBS.
2. *Ibid*.
3. Colbey Emmerson Reid and Dennis M Weiss, *Designing the Domestic Posthuman*, Bloomsbury, (London), 2024.
4. Genevieve Bell and Joseph Kaye, 'Designing Technology for Domestic Spaces: A Kitchen Manifesto', *Gastronomica* 2 (2), 2002, pp 46–62 at p 46.
5. *Ibid*.
6. Certain Measures website: https://certainmeasures.com/SBB-AUTONOMOUS-HOME, p 46.
7. *Ibid*.
8. Bell and Kaye, *op cit*, p 46.

Certain Measures, SBB Autonomous Home, Smart City Lab Basel, 2020

Reimagining the domestic field as a site of transit, here the architects dematerialise the smart home, envisioning it as an electric and networked metropolis of services and furniture in which autonomous appliances and personal belongings orbit the occupant.

The notion of the domestic posthuman seeks to challenge conventional cultural perceptions of current utilisation and potential approaches for the use of networked information technology within the home

Text © 2024 John Wiley & Sons Ltd. Images: pp 52–3, 61 Images courtesy Certain Measures; p 54(t) © Ross Sawyers; p 54(b) jeffwilcox, Creative Commons Attribution 2.0 Generic (CC BY 2.0); p 55 Courtesy of the artist; pp 56–7 © BETA Office; pp 58–9 © Whisker; p 60 © big-picture

Andrew Witt

ALIENS AMONG US
THE POSTHUMAN *WUNDERKAMMER*

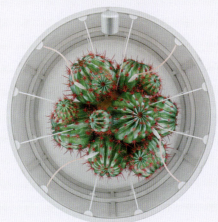
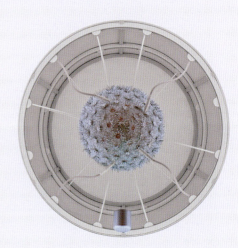

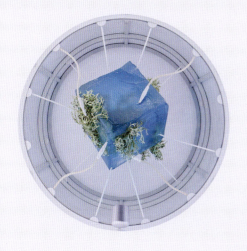

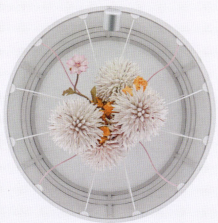

Certain Measures,
The Observatory,
Museum of the Future,
Dubai,
United Arab Emirates,
2022

Nine samples of physical maquettes of speculative species incubated in the Observatory. Over 80 imagined species are drawn from major global biomes such as aquatic, desert, forest and grassland.

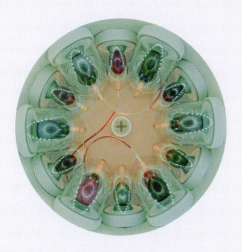

Architecture has always been about the reconciliation between humanity and matter. Nowadays, as we gear up for a posthuman future, should buildings and spaces be more proactive, challenging their users by asking questions about this multifaceted reconciliation between the biosphere and the ever more advanced technosphere? Harvard University's **Andrew Witt**, a co-founder of design studio Certain Measures, describes some of the office's ideas and spatial experiments within these trans-scalar environments and contexts.

In *Architecture, Animal, Human: The Asymmetrical Condition* (2006), architectural theorist Catherine Ingraham hints that geometry, wrestling with living matter, gives birth to architecture. Paraphrasing physicist Erwin Schrödinger, 'architecture has belonged, since the Renaissance, to both mathematics, "the physicist's most dreaded weapon," and life, which is "too involved to be fully accessible to mathematics."'[1] These two disciplinary forces – the mathematical and the biological, transcendent geometry and unruly life – interweave in the definition and generation of human space. Yet the duet of the mathematical and biological does not fully capture the modern state of these sciences, which has mutated and expanded beyond their classical definitions. Over recent years, the scientific primacy of mathematics has been superseded by data and information, and the science of life has mutated into synthetic biology and genetic engineering. To update Ingraham's line of thought, contemporary architecture would be born not purely of mathematics and biology but more specifically of data and genetics. At their nexus, a rich, complex and fertile ground is waiting for architecture to plant and cultivate.

Data and genetics offer designers calipers and scalpels with which to measure, describe and engage agents well beyond the human, extending to plants, animals, fungi, bacteria, artificial intelligence (AI) and techno-biological hybrids. By harnessing biological data and genetic code, architects could imagine computationally mediated collective environments for more-than-human flora and fauna alien from ourselves. Architecture could be a matrix of imbricated multispecies environments modulated by computation, and buildings could become engines for dimensioning, imaging and accelerating a flourishing tomorrow.

A Planetary View

The Observatory, a new experiential space for Dubai's Museum of the Future, hints at the potential of architecture to fuse bioengineering and AI in new multispecies environments. The project, developed by the design office Certain Measures and opened in 2022, proposes architecture as multi-scalar ecology of diverse and vital more-than-human intelligences nurtured through an AI-mediated human-machine hybrid Institute. Through its worldbuilding and transdisciplinary design, the Observatory argues for an expansive view of posthuman architecture teeming with biological and technological life. In so doing, it invites architects to embrace a new level of trans-scalar thinking that extends from the biological to the planetary.

The Museum of the Future imagines the world of 2071, presenting visitors with an empowering view of tomorrow. Each floor is a meticulously researched environment from that future. From an Earth-orbiting space station to the sensory spa of tomorrow, the museum engages technical, social, environmental and even spiritual themes through spatial means. The HEAL Institute, a fictional multinational non-governmental organisation (NGO) tasked with regenerating Earth's global ecology and cultivating a resilient biosphere, comprises the fourth floor of the museum. In response to climate change and the allied environmental catastrophes, the HEAL Institute gathers genetic material from the world's species, recombines this material into robust new organisms to resist climate extremes, and deploys those species around the world for strategic bioremediation. As the culmination of the HEAL Institute experience, the Observatory presents the results of this multispecies revitalisation project coming to fertile fruition. A hybrid of cryptozoologic natural history museum and information datascape, the Observatory imagines how data microcosm and biological macrocosm can merge in one architectural experience.

Over recent years, the scientific primacy of mathematics has been superseded by data and information, and the science of life has mutated into synthetic biology and genetic engineering

---

opposite top: Perspective of the Geoscope, a multi-scalar and panoramic media architecture that combines physical maquettes with a networked view of planetary ecology. Revealing the rhythms of life from bacteria to megaflora, the Geoscope presents a systemic and interconnected world picture.

opposite bottom: Detail view of the Geoscope showing symbiotic interrelationships between speculative species. The Geoscope's trans-scalar visualisation progressively scans Earth for emerging environmental challenges and monitors species as they regreen the planet.

Earth's Control Room

The Observatory is a dyad of two symbiotic sections: the Geoscope, a planetary-scale biomonitoring data visualisation, and the Nursery, a collection of accelerated growth incubators for engineered species. The Geoscope references Richard Buckminster Fuller's series of similarly titled immersive devices for dynamic mapping of Earth. Fuller's proposed Geoscope was a large geodesic dome covered in a dense matrix of computer-addressable lights capable of displaying 'various, accurately positioned, proportional data regarding world conditions, events, and resources'.[2] It was 'an instrument that can inform humanity about its invisibly trending evolutionary challenges – and do so in time to allow them to satisfactorily anticipate and cope with inexorable events'.[3] While Fuller's vision of planetary resources was extractive and human-centric, the Observatory offers a regenerative and more-than-human view of a return from the brink of ecological catastrophe. A constellation of portholes peer onto detailed physical maquettes of designed species, footage of HEAL Institute scientists delicately gathering field specimens, or rendered videos of the speculative species thriving in their new homes dispersed across Earth. Across the planetary datascape, an AI monitors specific metrics such as sea ice remediation level, microplastic density and atmospheric carbon density. Over time, the Geoscope slowly unfurls a graphic web of life, charting vital interdependencies between species, biomes, climates and planet. In a sense, the Geoscope is a control room for the planet, conducting orchestral variations on a theme of a blossoming world.

Opposite the Geoscope is the Nursery, a constellation of accelerated growth incubators that nurture species designed and engineered at the HEAL Institute. Nearly 80 physical models – carefully crafted to the fastidious standards of natural-history-museum maquettes – occupy domed vitrines, each species gestating for its deployment across the globe. A shimmering multitude of microcosms, the arrangement recalls Peter Sloterdijk's notion of foam: 'The guiding morphological principle of the polyspheric world we inhabit is no longer the orb, but the foam [...] In foam worlds, the individual bubbles are not absorbed into a single, integrative hyper-orb, as in the metaphysical conception of the world, but rather drawn together to form irregular hills.'[4] In this biological topography, species such as fire-resistant trees, soil-detoxifying mycelia or irrigation worms are represented in high-resolution detail, each contributing to a menagerie of synthesised life. Of course, the bioengineering can carry risks as well – an inadvertently invasive species, an unintended superpredator. The Observatory acts as a check for monitoring these potentially ill effects and sustaining a dynamic equilibrium.

Underpinning the graphic, modelled and narrative elements of the Observatory, an extensive technical infrastructure renders these fictions more visceral and tangible. Within the incubator pods, choreographed LED lighting subtly conveys the pulsing rhythms of incubation and growth. Transparent liquid-crystal (LCD) screens

> Over time, the Geoscope slowly unfurls a graphic web of life, charting vital interdependencies between species, biomes, climates and planet

Three states of the perpetually dynamic web of life presented by the Geoscope, which unfurls the interconnections between microbiome, biome and megabiome, showing the unique place of speculative species embedded within them.

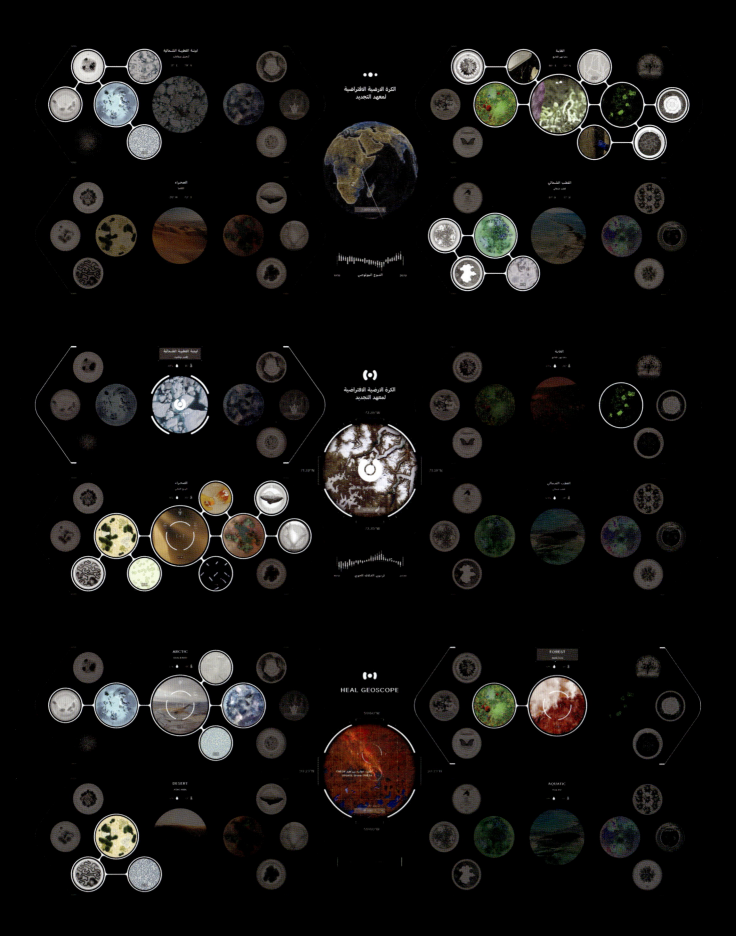

display evanescent quasi-holographic data visualisations of nascent vital signs, overlaid on the maquettes. These diaphanous visualisations count down the time to species maturity and deployment in their target biomes. An ambient soundscape performs a posthuman symphony of leaves rustling, insects chirping, machinery whirring and life growing. This is an architecture of complete sensation, conceived centrifugally from a posthuman *Wunderkammer* (cabinet of curiosities) of new species, a hive not for one kind of life but for life itself.

> The Observatory assembles a world as much as it represents one, and it draws on a centuries-long history of world architecturalisations through coordinated media

A Biotechnical World Image

To return to Catherine Ingraham's opening meditation, spaces like the Observatory prompt fundamental questions about the entanglements between technosphere and biosphere. 'We usually speak of the difference between the technical and biological as self-evident. But Schrödinger suggests that since both physical structures in space, such as buildings, and the physical body of living beings must accord with the physical laws of space we can, and should, bring these "objects" into the same space and compare their operations.'[5] In that spirit of collection, the Observatory assembles a world as much as it represents one, and it draws on a centuries-long history of world architecturalisations through coordinated media. It is an organic extension of 'polyvision' media architectures that synchronise myriad simultaneous image and video projections as coherent environments. Film historian Janine Marchessault argues that the emergence of multiscreen environments in the 1960s was connected with a 'desire to create world images', a totalising reconstruction that polyvision could uniquely provide.[6] Simultaneous channels of interrelated but distinct information streams juxtaposed to collage together a coherent portrait of a complex, roiling and multifarious whole.

The Observatory is a place to sense a newly emergent kind of nature but also a place in which to sense the shift in the human role within our world, and perhaps even to sense the transformation from human to posthuman. In his book *Posthuman Architecture*, architect and theorist Jacopo Leveratto argues that 'the most relevant thing that architectural design can do, if meant as a critical tool, when dealing with the emergence of the posthuman condition [...] is] not simply building working habitats for other subjects, but rather creating resonance chambers that challenge, step by step, the centrality of the human position in the present and future pictures of the planet'.[7] Indeed, the Observatory might be seen as precisely one of these resonating chambers: a space to imagine an alterity that embeds humans, AIs, natural and synthesised species, technosphere and biosphere in a common and interdependent matrix, a superorganism in which the architect not only designs a space but grows a new world. 𐐃

Notes
1. Catherine Ingraham, *Architecture, Animal, Human: The Asymmetrical Condition*, Routledge (New York), 2006, p 2.
2. R Buckminster Fuller, *The Critical Path*, St Martin's Press (New York), 1981, p 167.
3. Ibid, p 163.
4. Peter Sloterdijk, *Bubbles: Spheres I*, Semiotext(e) (Los Angeles), 2011, p 71.
5. Ingraham, *op cit*, p 3.
6. Janine Marchessault, *Ecstatic Worlds: Media, Utopias, Ecologies*, MIT Press (Cambridge, MA), 2017, p 3.
7. Jacopo Leveratto, *Posthuman Architecture: A Catalogue of Archetypes*, ORO Editions (Novato, CA), 2021, p 218.

Detail view of the Nursery, a constellation of incubator pods with holographic transparent liquid crystal displays (LCDs) that showcase speculative genetically engineered species. These displays show incubation time and include dynamic data visualisations of the unusual properties that make the species robust and resilient in their respective biomes.

Text © 2024 John Wiley & Sons Ltd.
Images courtesy Certain Measures.

Sylvia Lavin

Alternate Architectural Subjects

An Apple Tree That Lived on Long Island

Exploring how the human became a troublesome concept, **Sylvia Lavin**, Professor of History and Theory of Architecture at Princeton University, takes us to Long Island, where a house was rearranged by an unlikely inhabitant – an apple tree. While trees have typically served to reflect and reinforce idealised definitions of the human, the architecture made for this tree shortly after the Second World War suggests instead how interspecies relations were already pointing towards architecture beyond humanity.

> It is remarkable how closely the history of the apple-tree is connected with that of man.
> — Henry David Thoreau, 1862[1]

It is now widely accepted that 'the human' is a highly plastic concept under continual redefinition and redesign. The notion that human exceptionalism is both theoretically unsustainable as well as politically unethical is just as widely agreed upon. And equally uncontested is the fact that modern techniques for improving both the species and its dominion over the Earth have caused unimaginable violence. This hard-won consensus emphasises not only the need to do more than reinscribe and thus reinforce the enormous power given to the term 'human', but also that the prefix 'post-' does more than extend this claim to sovereignty beyond the present and into the future.

In other words, in addition to projecting notions of the human forward, it is worth considering when and under what circumstances architecture has already confronted its fragile instabilities and monstrous claims; to examine what conditions triggered architects to be attentive to the presumed cultural, biological and economic hierarchies that architecture has naturalised as intrinsically human; and to investigate what alternative decisions architects made or did not make as they learned about architecture's role in hominisation and considered alternate architectural subjects.

Tree House

The far eastern end of Long Island, New York, a few miles north of where German U-boat number 202 landed in 1942 as Operation Pastorius sought to disrupt the US conversion of natural resources like aluminium into armaments by sending saboteurs to strategic factories, is a case in point. There, postwar recovery entailed not only the rehousing of soldiers, the development of a consumer-driven economy and other historiographical commonplaces of the period, but the

```
Bernard Rudofsky and Costantino Nivola,
Nivola House-Garden,
Amagansett,
New York,
1950
```

One of the three open-air structures that together composed the outdoor house Rudofsky designed in collaboration with and for Costantino Nivola. This freestanding wall was built by Nivola in 1949 around an existing apple tree. Although often romanticised as evidence of a postwar return to nature, the wall/tree dyad was described by Rudofsky as a mediating apparatus through which shifting environmental conditions were projected as visualised information.

construction of a house for an apple tree in Amagansett – a collaborative undertaking by Italian sculptor Costantino Nivola and architect, curator and writer Bernard Rudofsky, commonly referred to as the Nivola House-Garden (1949–1950).

Nivola's and Rodofsky's centring of architecture around a tree, which still and increasingly serves as a stand-in for humans, and an apple tree in particular, which has historically served as an alibi for the cognitive capacities used to establish human superiority over all other forms of life, is typically understood as an effort to redirect modernity by restoring the balance between man and nature on the one hand, and man and technology on the other. Indeed, Rudofsky's portrait of the tree, captured in a photograph he took circa 1950, seems to frame it as a primitive and ethnographic subject who naturally generates a mural, thereby imparting what Ada Louise Huxtable, the architecture critic for the *New York Times*, described as an 'individualized warmly human touch […] on "cool" standardized, impersonal construction'.[2]

This type of integration of art and architecture became a central cultural and political preoccupation of many artists and architects during the 1950s, especially those whose lives were permanently rearranged by the war. According to this narrative, the postwar resurrection of humanism was enacted on Long Island because the apple tree, the pictorial arts and the human stood integrated as one actor to assert reassuring and rightful control over both nature and culture.

However, like the human bodies redesigned by modern clothing that Nivola sculpted in plaster as exhibition models for 'Are Clothes Modern?', curated by Rudofsky and held at the Museum of Modern Art (MoMA), New York, in 1944–5,[3] and like Rudofsky's photograph that stills and hence distorts the conditions of the tree's natural life, mid-century apples had been denatured by a complex of human and nonhuman actions. Brought to the US by English and Huguenot settlers in the early 17th century, one of the first immigrant apple seedlings was planted on Long Island. When grown from seeds rather than by grafting, a process whereby part of one plant is inserted into another to create a true duplication, hybrid variations prevail in the *Malus pumila*. As a result, over 17,000 varieties developed, leading the US Department of Agriculture (USDA) to establish a programme to document them by commissioning a series of photo-realistic watercolours. The uncanny images of the pomological collection minimised any trace of disturbance caused by the convergence of technological and natural reproduction, and inserted apples into a part machine- and part human-made signifying system.

Bertha Heiges,
Long Island Russet,
US Department of Agriculture
Pomological Watercolor Collection,
1905

opposite: In an effort both to document the many thousands of genetic variations of the fruit trees brought to the US by European settlers, as well as to develop scientific means of determining which were most amenable to the industrial farming that would eventually reduce the number of commercially available varieties to roughly four, in 1886 the US Department of Agriculture began commissioning artists to produce the Pomological Watercolor Collection. The images, like the fruit they represented, are techno-naturalistic hybrids: hand-made watercolours, painted to imitate photographs.

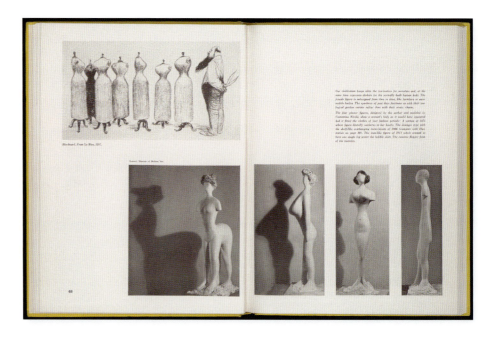

Bernard Rudofsky and Costantino Nivola,
Plaster figures,
'Are Clothes Modern?' exhibition,
Museum of Modern Art (MoMA),
New York,
1944-5

Spread from the accompanying publication. In a classic demonstration of the reconfiguration of the human body by cultural technologies, Nivola sculpted these models, designed by Rudofsky, showing a woman's body as it would have appeared had it fitted into the clothes of four fashion periods (1875, 1904, 1913 and the 1920s).

> **The postwar resurrection of humanism was enacted on Long Island because the apple tree, the pictorial arts and the human stood integrated as one actor to assert reassuring and rightful control over both nature and culture**

At the same time, trains and cold storage encouraged urbanites to develop an appetite for eating apples, leading them, along with Nivola, Rudofsky and German would-be saboteurs, to take the Long Island Railroad into New York. To compete in the urban market where food was chosen from a shelf rather than a tree, apples were given a glossy veneer sometimes made of wax, sometimes of kerosene, which horticulturalists nevertheless called a 'nickel-plate fancy'. By the late 1940s, in other words, apples – along with ducks, also immigrants to the US that first arrived from China in 1873, two of which, often referred to as Adam and Eve, adapted so well to Long Island that the eventual 70 tonnes of excrement produced daily by their descendants became one of the first targets of toxic clean-up on the island – had been redesigned inside and out and unmasked the Garden of Eden as a laboratory for the design of life.

The Collins Brothers with
George Reeve, John Smith
and Merlin Yeager,
'The Big Duck',
Flanders, New York,
1931

'The Big Duck,' a shop selling ducks farmed on Long Island, became famous to architects in 1977 when Robert Venturi and Denise Scott Brown used its image in *Learning from Las Vegas* to represent how modern functionalism had accidentally turned into symbolism. Not just images, however, ducks had by then become components of an intense industry, large enough to produce bio-waste in quantities that threatened the burgeoning postwar coastal real-estate market. Duck farming collapsed under the regulation that resulted, and 'The Big Duck', after being moved several times, is now a duckless tourist attraction.

Costantino Nivola, Cover of *American Cookery*, November 1945

Although this magazine cover designed by Nivola recalls a long tradition of still-life painting featuring dead animals, by 1945 most Americans acquired their holiday turkeys not by hunting or farming, but in a supermarket as a processed product. The turkey industry rapidly expanded after the Second World War, largely because developments in turkey architecture, particularly the design of brooder and finishing housing, lowered costs and increased output.

If Long Island had never been a garden it had certainly become an agricultural territory in which the distinctions between architecture and garden, culture and nature, human and nonhuman broke down. Apple trees, among the very first European settlers, had played a pivotal role in the dispossession and privatisation fundamental to the agriculturisation process, and been genetically modified in the process. Their remarkable adaptability, key to their long survival and almost planetary distribution, also explains why various human cultures had used apples as objects of psychic projection, converting them into potent religious symbols and epistemic models. By mid-century, this history shaped the way apples were again redesigned by contact with modern communication systems made of trains, shiny wax and watercolour, triggering yet another shift that demonstrates how the genus *Malus pumila* and the specimen on Long Island ended up as exemplars of post-life subjects and the architectures they engendered.

Architecture Rearranged

Nivola had a long and biographical connection with the elemental wall culture of Sardinian nuraghe (ancient megalithic edifices), and Rudofsky started bringing trees into architecture in the 1930s, following examples set by architects like Karl Friedrich Schinkel and Le Corbusier, but the wall they built through their collaboration together and with Long Island was directed just as much by the apple tree as by inherited architectural aesthetics and values. The wall came to the tree, not the other way around, determining its orientation and the location of its aperture. The tree/wall created a microclimate triggering a rearrangement of the house around minimal materials and maximal temperature gradients, from the single heat-absorbing wall to a four-walled solarium in which radiation quadrupled the temperature, to a structure for fire and pergola for shade. In other words, the result of the decisions made by Nivola and Rudofsky was success where the saboteurs failed; they interrupted the conventional conversion of resources into tools of land dispossession and biological hierarchy, a process often called architecture, and allowed the tree to blow the roof off the house and sabotage normative domestic programmes. The result was not a house where art and nature warmed cold materials to achieve a standard equated with human comfort, but a range of spatially distributed zones defined by temperature gradients from cool to hot.

Nivola and Rudofsky acted in an imaginative confrontation with this apple tree and, in so doing, revealed the rich possibilities made available by addressing something other than human as an architectural subject. Rudofsky, at least, recognised that this approach would not only decentre but also remake the human: writing about the house, he argued: 'No doubt man was well along his path when he knew how to make tools […] but […] he was still living in natural caves. By erecting his first free-standing wall he arrived at a point in his evolution that was as sharply defined as when he got up from all fours and stood on his legs. Building his first wall, he became, mentally, a biped […the wall] defines the beast.'[4]

Notes
1. Henry David Thoreau, 'Wild Apples', *The Atlantic Monthly* X (LXI), November 1862, p 513.
2. Ada Louise Huxtable, 'Art in Architecture 1959', *Craft Horizons* 19 (1), January/February 1959, p 13.
3. See the companion publication: Bernard Rudofsky, *Are Clothes Modern? An Essay on Contemporary Apparel*, Paul Theobald (Chicago, IL), 1947.
4. Bernard Rudofsky, 'The Bread of Architecture', *Arts and Architecture* 69 (10), 1952, p 28.

Text © 2024 John Wiley & Sons Ltd. Images: pp 70–71 Courtesy of Getty Research Institute, Los Angeles (920004). © DACS 2023; p 72 Digital image, The Museum of Modern Art, New York / Scala, Florence. © DACS 2023; p 73 US Department of Agriculture Pomological Watercolor Collection. Rare and Special Collections, National Agricultural Library, Beltsville, MD 20705; p 74(l) © Jon Bilous / Shutterstock; pp 74–5 Family of Costantino Nivola

Paul Dobraszczyk

BEYOND DOMESTICITIES

POSTHUMAN ARCHITECTURES FOR ANIMALS WE FARM

Design With Company (Stewart Hicks and Allison Newmeyer),
Farmland World,
2011

below: Imagining a theme park based on modern factory-farming methods, the architects' 'livestock Disneyland' features outsized animal-shaped machines such as a Cow Combine and Chicken Planter.

opposite: Two Cow Combines at work in Farmland World, as seen by a passing visitor.

Ever more astounding numbers of animals are being farmed for human consumption. **Paul Dobraszczyk**, a lecturer at the Bartlett School of Architecture, University College London, argues that humanity does not see or bother to comprehend the cruelty these animals are subjected to within industrialised farming processes and slaughterhouses. This, he says, is a design issue, requiring more effort to be made to give these animals a dignified life.

According to a 2019 report by the World Economic Forum, a combined total of 19 billion chickens, 1.5 billion sheep and 1 billion pigs are living at any one time on the planet: almost three times higher than the number of people.[1] Nearly all of these animals are destined for human consumption and every one has to be housed in some way. Whether or not we choose to call this 'architecture', it is mostly comprised of strictly utilitarian buildings, part of the factory-farm system that has developed rapidly in the Global North since the end of the Second World War.

A legitimate question we might ask is: do we want to extend our empathy towards these animals? This kind of posthuman leap is probably beyond the pale for many, excepting those who either choose not to eat animals or use animal-based products at all, or others who consider carefully the treatment of animals that produce their food or comestibles. There is good reason for the vast majority of buildings constructed to house livestock being hidden from the public gaze, whether the factory farms themselves or the terminal architecture of slaughterhouses. Some animal activists, like American writer Temple Grandin, have sought to intervene in end-of-life design for livestock. After visiting over 400 slaughterhouses in 20 countries, Grandin published a series of detailed design proposals for the improvement of animal welfare, such as non-slip floors and curvilinear chutes in slaughterhouses so that animals cannot see too far ahead.[2] These brave enquiries into spaces and structures most people would rather not even think about challenge commonplace ignorance of the levels of welfare of animals destined for human consumption.

Cow Country

In 2021, filmmaker Andrea Arnold released her documentary *Cow*, based on the life of a Holstein Friesian cow named Luma and her unnamed calf.[3] Filmed on a fairly typical English dairy farm in Kent – the county in which Arnold was born – Luma is shown living out her days in spaces dominated by colossal machines to which she is connected in a perpetual cycle of pumping, impregnation, gestation and birth. Like the majority of dairy cows, Luma is kept pregnant to continually produce milk; and all of this machinery is housed, alongside her, in a barn strewn with hay and copious bodily fluids. Luma's daily existence is regulated by a panoply of metal bars, chutes, grates, feeding troughs and pumping machines. Meanwhile, her estranged calf is initially raised in isolation – in a modular structure in a nearby field. Throughout the film, humans are present and although no direct cruelty is ever shown towards the cows, the entire system of farm architecture seems designed to eviscerate any familial connections between mother and calf in order to force both into a life of servitude in an entirely human-dominated environment.

It is easy to turn away from the animals reduced to livestock in this way, but there are perhaps more creative ways of engaging with these troubling subjects. In 2011, Stewart Hicks and Allison Newmeyer of Chicago-based

Ensamble Studio
(Antón García-Abril and Débora Mesa),
Trufa (Truffle),
Candamo, Spain,
2010

above: This house on Spain's Galician coast was in part created by the actions of a cow, who literally ate out the straw-filled interior to create its cavernous spaces.

opposite: Photomontage of the completed Trufa, showing its cavernous interior converted into a holiday home.

practice Design With Company proposed the creation of Farmland World, a chain of agro-tourist resorts built across the American Midwest in which guests would gain hands-on experience of contemporary farming practices. But Farmland World is not intended to be some kind of back-to-nature eco-retreat; rather, it is a spectacularly absurd development that would, in the architects' words, draw attention to the 'animal-machine hybrids'[4] that we see so clearly represented in *Cow*. These 'livestock Disneylands' would see visitors engaging with both real animals and also a range of outsized robotic machines that would enable them to perform modern practices of agriculture. Thus riding the Cow Combine, you would harvest crops through its mouth which would then be processed in a series of mechanical internal organs, rather like the multiple stomachs of a real cow. The processed crops would then be taken to storage buildings scattered across the site. Similar fun could be had driving an outsized Pig Plough, Sheep Baaaler, Goat Forage Harvester, Chicken Planter and Horse Manure Spreader.

Farmland World scales up the ways in which livestock like cows are increasingly controlled by machines, drawing attention to the absurdity of such a situation.

But we might also question the basic utilitarian understanding of cows that underlies modern farming systems. Perhaps cows can do something for themselves in this nightmarish world of control. The Trufa (Truffle) project, by Antón García-Abril and Débora Mesa of the Spanish practice Ensamble Studio, completed in 2010, turned the question of animal agency in architecture on its head. For the interior of this house was quite literally created by a cow named Pauline, who ate out what would become living spaces for humans (a holiday home for a private client). To begin with, a hole was dug in the ground and then filled with bales of hay. Reinforced concrete was then poured in around the edges and a hole was cut to allow Pauline to come and go as she pleased. Over the course of a year, this cow consumed the hay, leaving behind a grotto-like structure, the uneven concrete walls all that was left after Pauline had had her fill. Over that year, Pauline grew from a calf into a full-sized cow, while the space inside the house was gradually excavated; a very pleasing balance of accumulation and loss that perhaps speaks more strongly to issues of sustainability in architecture than any number of green walls.[5]

Pig City

In October 2022, the world's largest pig farm opened on the outskirts of Ezhou, a city in China's Hubei province. What was unusual about this particular pig farm was not its huge size but rather the fact that it was located in a 26-storey skyscraper. Another identical building will soon house more pigs (650,000 in total), the entire complex featuring temperature-, gas- and ventilation-controlled conditions. The animals are fed through more than 3,000 automatic troughs, the touch of a button from the central control room releasing their food when required. Waste is taken away in drains and then used to generate biogas which powers the pumps for the buildings' water supply.[6] Only two decades ago, this kind of animal architecture was the stuff of science fiction: MVRDV's speculative Pig City project in 2000 proposed a countryside network of similar towers to replace the existing land-hungry pork industry in the Netherlands. At the time, Pig City seemed like a satirical take on factory farming, upping the ante of utilitarian thinking to absurd levels of dystopian futurism.

With China's vertical pig farm, that future has now arrived, a consequence of the country's extraordinarily high demand for pork, but also of a more general acceptance of the benefits of vertical farming, as argued in Dickson Despommier's book *The Vertical Farm* (2010).[7] Yet, the costs are also high. Because of its intention to create a closed system of animal husbandry, even the human workers at China's vertical pig farm have to be incarcerated – with week-long shifts being reported for those who are given clearance to enter the building. Thus, what is posthuman here is more complex than simply an intensified technological control of livestock; human farmers themselves have become dehumanised as a result of their domination by the technologies of closed-loop production. Moreover, even the desired closed loop is a pernicious fantasy: there are always places in the system where control breaks down and leakages occur. For example, waste cannot be endlessly recycled – it eventually has to be removed in one form or another; disease is much more likely in a closed environment, and there is no guaranteed way of preventing its spread beyond the confines of the buildings. Finally, a high-rise pig farm may seem like a rational architectural solution to the increasing demand for pork, but it is no solution at all when it comes to developing more humane ways of living alongside the animals we choose to consume.

It is in small-scale farming practices that this can best be achieved. Zagreb-based practice SKROZ have already developed a portfolio of projects that address animal welfare in livestock, including Chickenville constructed in Rakov Patok in Croatia in 2018, and the Eco Pig Farm completed in 2022 in Cret Viljevski in the Slavonian region of eastern Croatia. The latter was built to breed Slavonian black pigs, indigenous to this part of the country, but largely outnumbered today by factory-farmed pigs that do not require access to pasture.

SKROZ,
Eco Pig Farm,
Cret Viljevski,
Croatia,
2022

Croatian practice SKROZ challenge the idea that livestock farms are beneath the remit of architects. This eco pig farm in rural Slavonia is not only a sophisticated response to the local vernacular buildings but also a celebration of the utilitarian in design.

A high-rise pig farm may seem like a rational architectural solution to the increasing demand for pork, but it is no solution at all when it comes to developing more humane ways of living alongside the animals we choose to consume

SKROZ's design features two identical barns, each with timber lattice façades that naturally ventilate and light the pig pens within. The buildings themselves reflect the vernacular architecture of rural Slavonia, a design choice that is meant to connect this contemporary farm with a distinctive local heritage. At the same time, SKROZ have also emphasised that these are not merely aesthetic embellishments; rather, they are part and parcel of the rationalisation of the spaces and the optimisation of the breeding process.[8] With their modular pens and moveable partitions, the interiors of the barns reflect something of the utopian charge of architectural Modernism which saw standardisation as not primarily about efficiency but rather flexibility and freedom for inhabitants. Yet they also reject the conformism of Modernism in emphasising what might be described as an animal-centred version of what architect and historian Kenneth Frampton termed 'critical regionalism'.[9] In shifting the emphasis towards animals, SKROZ in effect sidestep some of the problems associated with Postmodernism in human-centred architecture, namely the tendency towards pastiche of historical styles at the expense of an authentic engagement with the local.

Chickenville

Around 70 billion chicken are slaughtered for food every year, and that number is rising fast, especially in rapidly industrialising countries like China and India.[10] That equates to over 2,000 chickens killed every second. No wonder that the animated film *Chicken Run* (2000)[11] portrayed a chicken factory farm as an animal concentration camp, replete with watchtowers, acres of barbed-wire fencing, ferocious guard dogs and punishments for would-be escapees (the chickens are always trying to escape). After many failed attempts, the chickens eventually build a makeshift aeroplane in which they fly off to a better free-range life. The analogy between chicken farm and concentration camp is apposite: of all livestock, factory-farmed chickens arguably have the worst lot in life, whether egg-producing hens (layers) or their male counterparts (broilers) destined to become our food. They live out their average 42-day existences in spaces smaller than an A4 piece of paper in gigantic sheds filled with tens of thousands of birds who never venture outside. Battery farms for egg-laying hens are even more horrific (the reason why they are banned in some countries): young females spend their short lives in cramped cages, with thousands of these lined up and stacked in vertical tiers.[12]

SKROZ's Chickenville aims to put people back in touch with chickens destined for human consumption. It is a poultry farm in rural Croatia that not only purports to produce eggs with zero carbon footprint but also to raise awareness, among the local population, of eco-friendly poultry-farming practices. In complete opposition to factory-farmed chickens, which are kept well hidden, SKROZ have opened up every stage of egg production to public scrutiny. The central zone in Chickenville enables both visitors' and farmers' access, without interrupting the farming function of the site. The chicken coops themselves use traditional materials (chicken wire and unfinished timber from fir trees) but are raised above the ground on metal stilts to create a protected, shaded area underneath for the chickens to roam and for farmers to easily access their eggs. Three of the four units house 25 hens and one rooster, an extraordinarily low density compared to conventional factory farms. The other unit houses a small number of broilers.[13]

Doug Argue,
Untitled,
1995

above: Argue's gigantic oil painting – measuring 366 by 549 centimetres (144 by 216 inches) – of an imagined factory farm for egg-laying chickens is by no means an exaggeration of the environmental conditions created by factory-farming methods.

SKROZ,
Chickenville,
Rakov Patok,
Croatia,
2018

right: With Chickenville, SKROZ challenge the idea that poultry farms should be kept out of the public eye: here, local people are actively welcomed in order for them to learn about more humane ways of keeping chickens for their eggs and meat.

More-than-Human Architecture

Chickenville restores dignity to the lives of its bird residents, despite the fact they are still very much under human control and serving entirely human ends. As with their more recent Eco Pig Farm, SKROZ demonstrate that we can still care for animals destined for our plates – that the instrumentalising of animals need not preclude us extending empathy towards them. This is a vital element in the project of creating a more-than-human architecture, particularly as buildings are so implicated in the modern factory-farming system, whether or not architects are involved in the design of cowsheds, milking parlours, pigsties or chicken coops. Can we ever imagine livestock actually taking pleasure in the buildings we design for them? In philosopher Timothy Morton's estimation, this is the challenge presented to us when it comes to post- and more-than-human architecture. In *Humankind* (2019), Morton argues that we need to cultivate kindness towards nonhumans in our approaches towards design, and to do it by trying to imagine our buildings from the perspectives of other animals.[14] If, as most pet-owners will likely agree, we can know what dogs and cats get pleasure from in our homes, why can we not sense the same for cows, pigs, chickens and other livestock? ∆

Notes
1. 'This is How Many Animals We Eat Each Year', World Economic Forum, 8 February 2019: https://www.weforum.org/agenda/2019/02/chart-of-the-day-this-is-how-many-animals-we-eat-each-year/.
2. Temple Grandin, 'Making Slaughterhouses More Humane for Cattle, Pigs, and Sheep', Department of Animal Science, Colorado State University, 2013: https://www.grandin.com/references/making.slaughterhouses.more.humane.html.
3. *Cow*, directed by Andrea Arnold, MUBI, 2021.
4. 'Farmland World', https://mascontext.com/issues/speed/farmland-world.
5. See https://www.ensamble.info/thetruffle for a short film of the project.
6. 'China's 26-Storey Pig Skyscraper Ready to Produce 1 Million Pigs a Year', *The Guardian*, 25 November 2022: https://www.theguardian.com/environment/2022/nov/25/chinas-26-storey-pig-skyscraper-ready-to-produce-1-million-pigs-a-year.
7. Dickson Despommier, *The Vertical Farm: Feeding the World in the 21st Century*, Thomas Dunne Books (London), 2010. The book was republished by Picador in 2020.
8. 'Eco Pig Farm', https://skroz.hr/projekti/farma-za-uzgoj-autohtonih-crnih-slavonskih-svinja/.
9. Kenneth Frampton, 'Towards a Critical Regionalism: Six Points for an Architecture of Resistance', in Hal Foster (ed), *The Anti-Aesthetic: Essays on Postmodern Culture*, Bay Press (Port Townsend, WA), 1983, pp 16–30.
10. See Paul Mundy (ed), *Meat Atlas 2021*, Heinrich Böll Stiftung (Berlin), 2021, p 21: https://friendsoftheearth.eu/wp-content/uploads/2021/09/MeatAtlas2021_final_web.pdf.
11. *Chicken Run*, directed by Peter Lord and Nick Park, Aardman Animations and DreamWorks Animation, 2000.
12. '10 Things You Should Know About Factory-farmed Chickens', World Animal Protection, 29 November 2016: https://www.worldanimalprotection.org/news/10-facts-you-should-know-about-factory-farmed-chickens.
13. 'Chickenville', https://skroz.hr/en/projekti/chickenville/.
14. Timothy Morton, *Humankind: Solidarity with Nonhuman People*, Verso (London), 2019, pp 143–4.

Text © 2024 John Wiley & Sons Ltd. Images: pp 76–7 © Design With Company; pp 78–9 © Ensamble Studio; pp 80–81, 82–3(b) © Bosnic+Dorotic; pp 82–3(t) Doug Argue, Creative Commons Attribution-Share Alike 4.0 International (CC BY-SA 4.0)

Steven Hutt

FLYING FERAL

POSTHUMAN ARCHITECTURES, ENCLOSURES AND OPEN-LOOP INTERFACE DESIGNS

Auke-Florian Hiemstra /
Naturalis Biodiversity Center,
Birds' nest,
Antwerp, Belgium,
2023

A birds' nest made by magpies outside a hospital in Antwerp. The nest has been constructed using anti-bird spikes woven into the structure. Eurasian magpies and carrion crows have found a way to dismantle the spikes and use them as a construction material. Similar nests have been spotted, which contain windscreen wipers, plastic carnations and condoms.

Architect and advocate of speculative posthuman ecological design **Steven Hutt** offers new thoughts on the integration of wildlife into our architectures and cities. Awareness of the 'feral' as a design tool, the push and pull between indigenous and non-indigenous species, and even old ideas of colonialism are all agents in this new posthuman landscape. There are many aspects of this often anti-anthropocentric worldview across a variety of scales. Might zoo animals one day be able to decide how we look at them and observe their habits?

Steven Hutt,
Feral Flyways,
2023

opposite: The Feral Flyways diagram speculates on the interwoven relationships of architectural projects, publications, designers, theorists and agencies that actively shape current feral discourse, and the flying-feral agents that thrive in our inter-situ posthuman landscapes. The three primary flight paths – 'Feral Architectures', 'Feral Literature' and 'Feral Agency' – entwine to highlight the complex sympoietic relationships that exist at the physical, metaphysical and epistemological borders of ferality over time.

Architecture and flying-feral territories have long been entangled – by design or, more often than not, by accident. China's Four Pests Campaign (1958) was brutal but short-lived. Chairman Mao encouraged his citizens to march in the streets and frighten feral Eurasian tree sparrows into ceaseless flight until they dropped dead of exhaustion. Troops even encircled the extraterritorial land of foreign embassies where the birds found temporary shelter, beating drums until the small corpses piled up. By eliminating sparrow populations (and rats, flies and mosquitoes), it was assumed China's rice yields would increase. Instead, the resulting ecological imbalance caused locust and other insect populations to grow exponentially, ravaging crops across the country. The resulting famine was largely responsible for the 35–50 million human deaths during Chairman Mao's Great Leap Forward (1958–62).[1]

Murmurations
Today, the feral birds that briefly inhabited our empty runways have retreated, as the fleeting freedoms offered by the disruptions of the Covid-19 pandemic wane. For billions of nonhuman entities, the pandemic was a veritable success. But our penchant for controlling feral airways has only escalated, albeit through increasingly sterile and hostile design solutions: metal spikes, electrified wire, netting, mirrors, chemicals, biological controls, genetic engineering, light pollution, magnetic fields and plastic birds of prey. And mirrored by the equally controlling deterministic agendas of biophilic protagonists. These agendas wield wholesale techno-fixes to restore particular native species with naive xenophobic fervour, citing the well-meaning conservation agendas of the International Union for Conservation of Nature (IUCN) Red List, World Wide Fund for Nature (WWF) and other bodies to substantiate speciesism, often with little meaningful engagement with ecologists or the more-than-human creatures they purport to champion. Architects and flying-feral species both share this strenuous relationship with conservation and preservation. Both are deeply entangled in historical, sociopolitical, technological, ecological, aesthetic and posthuman debate in relation to the frictions of urban and peri-urban landscapes – which forces post-dualistic narratives and aesthetics to emerge beyond the weary dichotomies of nature versus culture, wild versus domestic, and in-situ versus ex-situ.

But what does it mean to be feral? The word has antagonistic connotations, often linked with the humans and other unruly animals that scavenge on the fringes of our physical, social and metaphorical spaces. Recently, the term has been adopted by (re)wilding advocates to spark affirmative action, and by posthuman theorists such as Mel Y Chen[2] to challenge biopolitics and queer culture. Like a living intersect by artist Gordon Matta-Clark, these feral creatures directly challenge spatial narratives of architecture, both at the intimate borders of enclosure and at the wider scales of territorial flyways and urban ecosystems at large.

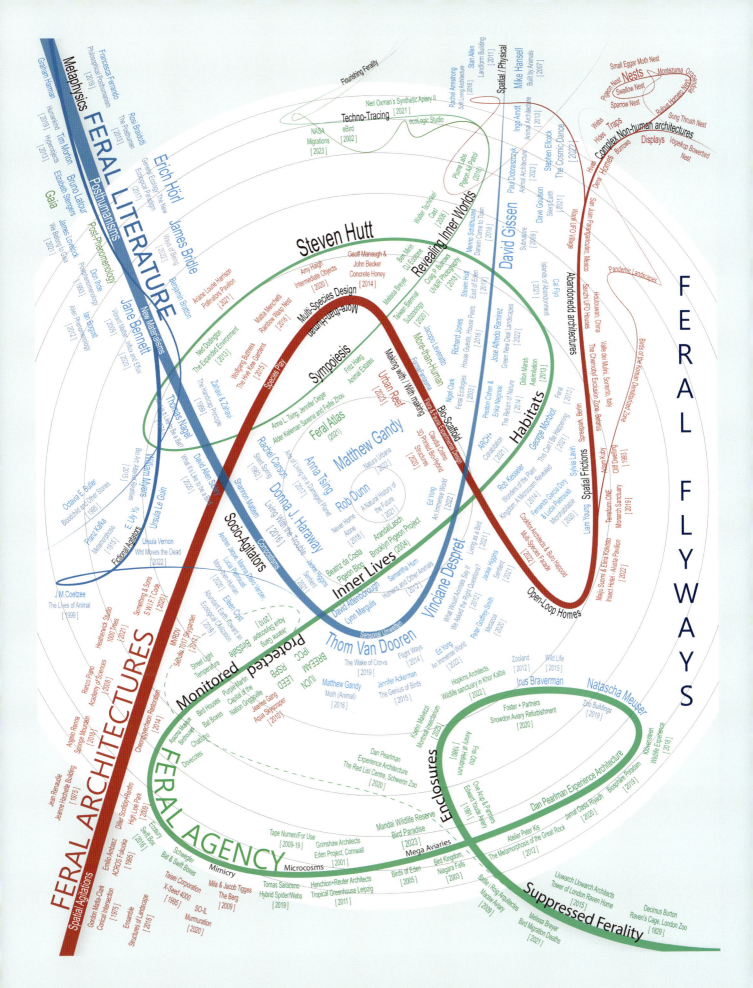

Pilots

Speculative architects citing more-than-human clients have largely piloted façade interface prototypes for synanthropes, following an early 21st-century boom in landform building, habitable roof landscaping and regulatory shifts for façades to reduce bird collisions. These discrete approaches retain the hermetically sealed human interior as distinctly 'separate from', yet their collective viability to challenge and transform existing ecosystems through 'architectural imprinting' is worth further exploration. The following prototypes represent two modes of interface design that move beyond low-fi primitivisms, to promote technologically complex open-loop systems for trans-species inclusivity.

The first, anthropomorphic 'home building', dates back approximately 10,000 years to our roots as domesticators, spawning innumerable aesthetic experiments over the centuries, ranging from the ornate stone birdhouses carved on the exterior of Istanbul's Ayazma Mosque (1757–61), to the tall, utilitarian pigeon towers of Cairo's crowded urbanscapes. The latest prototype for a load-bearing terracotta façade system, the Living Façade by COOKFOX Architects and Buro Happold (New York, 2022), offers a more expansive vision of cohabitation and aerospatial habitonomics. Spencer Lapp, lead designer and beekeeper, is experimenting with various modular scales, forms, colourations, textures and compositions to promote feral co-habitation. Within this ongoing project, one façade module promotes interactions with the many species of solitary bees that thrive in New York City. Another module, with a curved 1 9/16-inch (3.9-centimetre) opening, supports a multitude of small birds' nests. The design approach is overtly technical and actively considers ventilation, drainage, shading and protection, while simultaneously exploring the craft of curvaceous slip casting and glazing. The unseen rear of the façade may also be designed to support nocturnal species. Other overt homebuilding projects include Ariane Harrison's Pollinators Pavilion (New York, 2020) and Terreform ONE's Monarch Sanctuary (New York, 2019), a modular terrarium façade designed to host monarch butterflies.

COOKFOX Architects and Buro Happold,
Living Façade,
New York,
2022

opposite: A prototype for a ceramic multi-species façade system, designed with a series of modular self-regulating habitats that encourage co-living with small birds, solitary bees and other flying insects. The aesthetics are formed around aerospatial habitonomics, with openings and microclimates to attract New York City's local urban fauna.

below: This prototype for a 'living façade' system has been designed with complex curves and a deep profile, to increase distinct lines of shading throughout the day. The design team thus aim to minimise potential bird collisions with the glazed rear of the façade system.

Terraform ONE,
Monarch Sanctuary,
New York,
2019

The Monarch Sanctuary is a speculative tower that weaves butterfly conservation strategies into the façade of a commercial building in New York City. The diagrid structure is designed to be infilled with ETFE foil and glass, to form a terrarium and enclose a vertical ecosystem that helps monarch butterflies to thrive.

The second mode, 'scaffolding', takes a more hands-off approach. The Rotterdam-based team at Urban Reef are printing porous, labyrinthine 'reefs' to create environments suitable for life to take hold and flourish. The team use the Delta WASP 40100 ceramic 3D-printer technology, and Grasshopper 3D, to experiment with printable clay and organic composites to encourage biodiversity, anticipating that the formal aesthetics of their maze-like reefs will evolve alongside the limits of printing technologies and the structural limits of printable materials. Their iterative design-monitoring process is also deeply entangled within another worlding experiment: zoological design. These organic bio-scaffolds are being tested inside the controlled environments of the Amazonica Dome and Riviera Hall at Rotterdam Zoo. The team also monitor their growth systems alongside emerging biotechnologies at BlueCity Lab (Rotterdam), the first circular biolab of its kind.

To be both aerial and feral means to shape, co-evolve and thrive as a result of (and often in spite of) an elaborately interwoven sympoiesis[3] and symbiosis with humans, architectures, landscapes and the wider ecologies of space. Aerial evolutionary advantages span deep time, and fork across phylogenetic populations – from flying birds, bats and insects, to gliding squirrels, fish and even snakes. Flying/gliding species are ever adapting to fluctuations in air temperatures, turbulence and pressure, magnetic fields and star formations, lines of sight and lines of shite.[4] Architectural forms directly affect all of these. It is here that designers can engage with models of ecological responsibility, environmental justice and trans-species solidarity, and we must also challenge the social implications of post-biological flying-feral drones and nanotechnologies. How such designs will affect the future trajectories of bio/post-bio airborne species will unfurl in unknowable ways, but future modes of interface design need to focus on co-modification.

Urban Reef,
Rotterdam, The Netherlands,
2023

above: A series of 3D-printed labyrinths, installed onto the side of an existing façade, to provide shelter and space within which a range of living organisms might thrive. The openings of these prototypes form ideal cavities for smaller birds to nest in, but Urban Reef is a non-deterministic experiment that seeks to encourage any organism to interact with the spatial forms created.

right: A 3D-printed reef, designed with myriad labyrinthine forms, acts as a scaffold to encourage different forms of life to thrive within. The reef is printed in clay to absorb water, and provides a range of open-loop microclimates and nutrients for organisms to thrive in the city.

Designing sympoietically means more than simply acknowledging 'the other', or preserving known quantities in static states; it requires a continual critical awareness of co-making, co-designing and even rethinking the self

Steven Hutt,
Feral Aviary,
Edward Youde Aviary,
Hong Kong Park,
Hong Kong,
2019

A photograph of the sweeping border of stainless-steel mesh that divides the Edward Youde Aviary (Ove Arup & Partners, 2007) and Hong Kong Park. The netting keeps the critically endangered yellow-crested cockatoo out of confinement.

Descent

Yellow-crested cockatoos are critically endangered in Indonesia, with only 1,000 to 2,500 wild specimens left in their native habitat. But 3,000 kilometres away from 'home', in Hong Kong, they have recently found a foothold as feral agents. This urban 'crackle' now represents 10 per cent of their entire species. Outside the Edward Youde Aviary (Ove Arup & Partners, Hong Kong, 2007), they can be heard clacking provocatively at the 80 species of protected birds contained within.

Alienating discourse surrounding feral invasiveness and native descent reveals much about inherited colonial biases and xenophobia within a given territory, impacting whether the flying-feral will flourish or falter as cultural species, and forcing the question: Which forms of preservation still have a place within our posthuman landscapes? Designing sympoietically means more than simply acknowledging 'the other', or preserving known quantities in static states; it requires a continual critical awareness of co-making, co-designing and even rethinking the self.

Debates about zoological care systems rage on, not least in the highly spatial and architectural 'in-situ versus ex-situ' dualisms that continue to systematically institutionalise, naturalise, classify, register, regulate, prioritise, suppress and assert themselves on all species. They are linked with the territorial projects of (re)wilding, protected flight paths and green corridors – and embroiled within the philosophies, politics and promises of the inter-situ, the space 'in-between' which the feral has always inhabited. Zoological veterinarians increasingly rely on these in-between spaces to assist endangered species through multifarious shades of captivity. The inter-situ has therefore become a space of radical experimentation and debate (over what lives and dies by design), offering the potential for architects to create new techno-zoological responses.

The rapid evolution of zoos into educational institutions has also influenced significant advances in contemporary veterinary care and enclosure design. The evolution of cages, aviaries, greenhouses, butterfly houses, terrariums and insectariums reflects these new agendas. However, the entrenched anthropocentric categorisation of architectural dichotomies – interiors, enclosures, landscapes – and their associated omnipotent regulations is evolving more slowly, and not anywhere near fast enough to keep up with societal shifts.

This architectural lag is rendered in projects such as Hopkins Architects' Khor Kalba Turtle and Wildlife Sanctuary (Sharjah, UAE, 2022), designed as a series of interconnected precast-concrete pods displaying animals in distinctly museum-like conditions. Although Kühn Malvezzi's new Montreal Insectarium (2022) challenges the efficacy of zoomuseology – the design of its anthropomorphic routes mimics insect habitats – the focus is still on voyeuristic human experience. However, the 2021 refurbishment by Foster + Partners of the Grade II-listed Snowdon Aviary at London Zoo represents a step in the right direction. The structure has been transformed to house high-flying colobus monkeys. Sir David Attenborough suggested that to respect their privacy, zoos keep primates behind walls, with peepholes for visitors to look through rather than gawping through floor-to-ceiling glass panels.[5] A more alluring posthuman symbiotic approach might be to cede control of these peepholes, and other scopic interactive regimes, to the animals – seriously challenging the presuppositions of what constitutes a zoo experience.

The current generation of zoo architecture is more concerned with brand development at increasingly larger scales. The latest in a succession of mega-aviaries, Bird Paradise at Singapore's Mandai Wildlife Reserve (2023), is now the largest of its kind in Asia, hosting 3,500 birds from more than 400 species. Eight walk-through aviaries mimic different habitats from around the world. Landscaped with imported flora, these bioramas re-enact the familiar, static staging of a utopian Holocene. Meanwhile, a great hornbill flies through the 'scene' with a prosthetic 3D-printed rhinotheca. We ought to imagine a more techno-inclusive environment for this wondrous dinosaur-descendant-turned-cyborg, beyond the hubris of nature staging, to encourage agency through sensorial aerial interfaces, and the ability to alter environs using technological mediation such as AI imprinting.

Architect Natascha Meuser notes that zoo animals now represent their body doubles in the wild,[5] divorcing animals from environment. The next generation of zoos must acknowledge species and environments as four-dimensional, self-actualising assemblages. We need fewer body doubles, and more digital twins.

Landing
Ecologically posthuman architecture must ultimately encourage feral genius – and we must synthesise alien sensory umwelten with our human modes of experience.

Steven Hutt,
Frozen in Flight,
Munich Zoo Aviary,
Munich,
2022

opposite: Designed by Frei Otto in 1980, the aviary is built as a complex tent-like structure utilising thin stainless-steel mesh which suspends a blanket of snow above the space below after a heavy snowfall. The Munich Hellabrunn Zoo is recognised as the world's first 'GeoZoo', which is spatially planned according to the geographical origins of species. Many contemporary zoological gardens continue to use such spatial planning as a basis for zoo design.

Foster + Partners,
Snowdon Aviary,
London Zoo,
London,
2021

Foster + Partners' 2021 refurbishment of the Snowdon Aviary designed by Cedric Price, Antony Armstrong-Jones (1st Earl of Snowdon) and Frank Newby in 1962–4 has transformed the existing steel-meshed enclosure for birds into a new home for colobus monkeys. The firm designed a series of vertical elements and pulley systems within the space to encourage the monkeys to play, leap, jump and swing around the confines of the aviary.

Already, NASA analyses the interannual variability of bird migration to predict climate patterns. Plume Lab collect localised urban air-pollution data by strapping air-quality sensors to pigeons. We can easily imagine such technologies at an architectural scale. However, we should strive for a more-than-beneficial approach beyond housing and utility. A 2022 study published in the journal *Animal Behaviour* revealed that bumblebees can play.[7] How might an urban playground for bumblebees be (co-)designed and function? Ultraviolet-induced visible fluorescence (UVIVF) photographic techniques reveal the glowing fluorescence emitted by plants that insects, but not humans, can see. Architects should seriously consider using design drivers such as infrared and ultraviolet light, magnetic and electrical fields and echolocation, as embodied by artist Kolbeinn Hugi's visual arts project Animal Internet, which imagines a zoocratic future of neural interfaces and mediation by artificial intelligence, enabling animals to participate in human decision-making processes.[8]

More alluring still is the latent opportunity to challenge our kin biases through co-designing with the filthy, ugly, alien, dangerous undesirables that live among us, such as the mosquitos that now live in the London Underground (that are rapidly evolving to feed exclusively on humans). And with two-thirds of species now expanding their range north due to climate shifts, it is high time we untangle our native exceptionalisms to speculate instead on welcoming future feral flyways across our burning planet.

In the midst of our sixth – anthropogenic – mass extinction of our feral kin, we might even consider architectural abandonment as a form of ecological posthuman design. As we debate over what lives and dies by design while actively tinkering with species habitats, supporting the meek while suppressing the dangerous, we only compound speciesism in more elaborate ways. This reinscribes the long arm of humanism to flap its all-too-human appendage, in another fire of its own making. Dutifully fanning the flames, in a vain attempt to fly the worthy ones, and itself, off to some non-existent extraterritorial safe-house. ⌒

Notes
1. Judith Shapiro, *Mao's War Against Nature,* Cambridge University Press (Cambridge), 2001, pp 88–9.
2. Mel Y Chen, *Animacies: Biopolitics, Racial Mattering, and Queer Affect*, Duke University Press (Durham, NC), 2012.
3. See Donna Haraway, *Staying With the Trouble,* Duke University Press (Durham, NC), 2016.
4. Andrés Jaque, Marina Otero Verzier and Lucia Pietroiusti (eds), *More-than-Human*, Het Nieuwe Instituut (Rotterdam), 2020, p 49.
5. Sir David Attenborough, paraphrased interview on *Good Morning Britain*, ITV. First aired 17 October 2016.
6. Natascha Meuser, *Zoo Buildings*, DOM Publishers (Berlin), 2019.
7. Hiruni Samadi Galpayage Dona et al, 'Do Bumble Bees Play?' *Animal Behaviour* 194, December 2022, pp 239–51.
8. Animal Internet: https://animalinternet.earth.

Text © 2024 John Wiley & Sons Ltd. Images: pp 84–5 © Auke-Florian Hiemstra; pp 87, 91, 92(t) © Steven Hutt; pp 88, 89(l) © COOKFOX Architects and Buro Happold; p 89(r) © COOKFOX Architects and Buro Happold; p 90 © Urban Reef; pp 92–3(b) © Foster + Partners

Olga Bannova and Sandra Häuplik-Meusburger

LEARNING, TEACHING,

THE EVOLUTION OF SPACE ARCHI

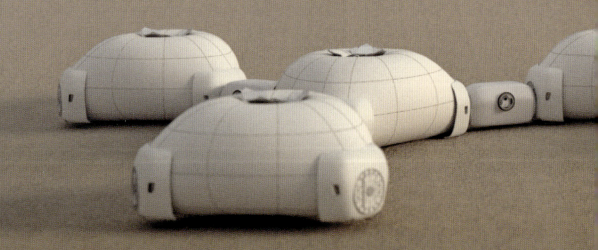

Miruna Vecerdi and Rudolf Neumerkel,
Project Adventus,
Mars Science City design studio,
Research Unit Building Construction and Design 2 (HB2),
TU Wien, Vienna, Austria,
2020

The habitat autonomously deploys when placed on the surface of Mars, providing a prompt and efficient living space. With additional modules it can be expanded into a larger base that integrates with the Martian landscape, optimising its form, function and materials to adapt to the in-situ conditions.

COEXISTING, THRIVING

TECTURE IN THE POSTHUMAN ERA

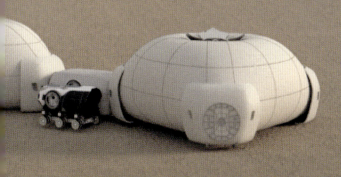

Olga Bannova directs the Sasakawa International Center for Space Architecture (SICSA) at the University of Houston, Texas, and **Sandra Häuplik-Meusburger** directs the Space Architecture EMBA at Vienna University of Technology (TU Wien). Here they present the notion of viewing humanity as not superior to other beings and entities, allowing the possibility of the much more inclusive coexistence that will be necessary as our posthuman future pushes us deeper into Space.

Navigating towards the future means engaging in open and meaningful discussions, recognising the challenges ahead, striving for excellence in our fields and incorporating one another's perspectives.

What is the human's and humanity's place in Space? Learning from experience and each other, space architecture educators and practitioners always explore the intricacies of different languages, methods and attitudes to benefit from the mindset of both an architect and engineer.[1] Recognising that there is no single right answer or perfect solution for solving all problems, either known or unforeseen, space architects perceive this truth as an opportunity rather than a hindrance. The lessons gleaned from the past do not provide ultimate answers, but rather teach architects and engineers an invaluable skill of listening and embracing the multitude of potential perspectives and ideas.

Desire to explore has always been part of human nature, and it was through following this desire that humans advanced beyond the boundaries of their homes and their home planet and into the 'final frontier' – Space. But there is so much to learn to make this exploration a rewarding and harmless experience for people and new worlds! How can a design experience on Earth be applied in the final frontier without repeating mistakes that were made before, or at least while minimising similar errors? Learning from different disciplines, cultures and societies helps to shift the design paradigm towards new strategies where reducing, reusing and recycling of all assets become a foundation of all design practices: not only on Earth but also in Space.

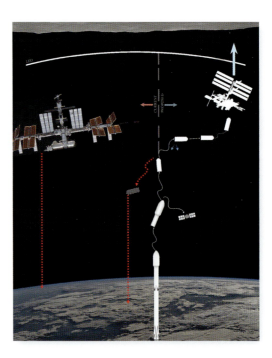

Ve.sh pavilion, Versatile Spaces design studio, Research Units Building Construction and Design 2 (HB2) and Structural Design and Timber Engineering (ITI), TU Wien, Vienna, Austria, 2023

Thinking out of the box and prototyping with new materials is triggered at the collaborative design studio series Versatile Spaces. In 2023, students crafted a versatile public architecture using recycled blinds and hosted a sustainability and reuse symposium.

Erin Quigley, '"Designed" Debris', Space Architecture Master's thesis, Sasakawa International Center for Space Architecture (SICSA), University of Houston, Texas, 2023

Better understanding of sustainable architectural practices on Earth helps to define space architecture design goals. Space architecture design strategy aims to reduce future orbital debris, reuse upper-stage rockets, and recycle materials and components for in-Space construction purposes.

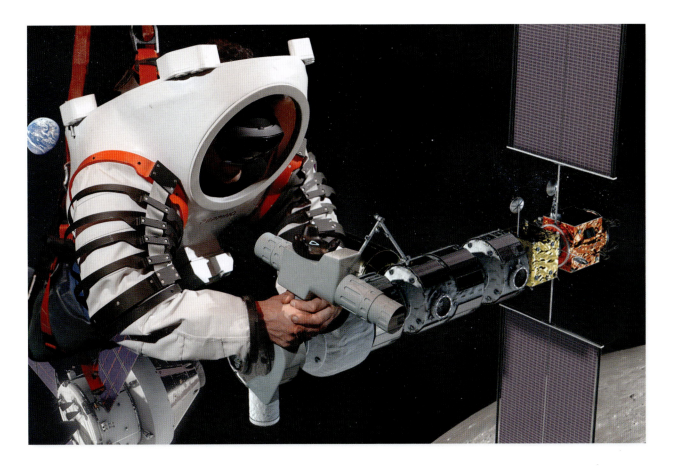

Design evaluation using virtual/mixed reality (VR/MR), Immersive Design and Validation Space (IDVS) Lab, Sasakawa International Center for Space Architecture (SICSA), University of Houston, Texas, 2023

Interactive processes and simulation technologies are becoming essential tools for design evaluation and validation for future human or posthuman Space missions.

Designing to Coexist with the Unknown

Coexisting philosophy applied to design practices refers to knowledge obtained from the history of gained experiences. In Space, humans will face more unknown factors than those that are already recognised as Space-flight-related circumstances. These new environments are hostile: the conditions are dangerous for humans and any living creatures that will be brought there, including plants. Discovering how to coexist in new worlds is just as important as creating protection and safety means that separate living environments from the surrounding world. Learning how to deal with the unknown, as well as how to coexist with various known factors, become critical skills for space architects: they need to acquire not only factual knowledge but also a sense of visionary thinking. Understanding the logic behind design and decision-making processes, and exploring creative approaches, equips architects with the necessary tools to navigate the challenges of their profession – both in Space and on Earth.

To make the design adjustable for the needs of future space explorers and unknowns of new environments, space architects must embrace the element of uncertainty associated with their work and find a way to adapt in order to survive and thrive in ever-evolving conditions and environments. Both humans, as individuals, and the environment itself need to undergo continuous adaptation for sustainable coexistence in Space. To develop new design strategies for Space projects, their architects need to find new ways of evaluating their designs in relation to human experiences during multiple levels of interactions between people, their equipment and their environment inside and outside their habitation.

As it transitions from coexistence to thriving, space architecture is embarking on a transformative path for the posthuman era. Amidst this shift, it is crucial for humans to retain humanity. The notion of posthumanity does not imply a world devoid of humans; rather, it signifies an environment that accommodates their needs alongside those of other living beings, different conditions and new realities. Recognising that humans are not superior to anyone or anything suggests harmonious coexistence with other existences. This pursuit of symbiosis is essential for thriving in the vast expanse of Space. By embracing empathy, respect and a deep understanding of the interconnectedness of all beings, space architecture can pave the way to a future where humanity and other forms of life can flourish together.

Coexistence can be applied to design strategy at different levels. It may help to rethink the design of structural elements such as protective walls where growing and living tissues can be combined with standard building materials to boost symbiotic efficacy. At a larger scale, the coexisting design strategy can lead to finding a way to benefit from settings that are present in new worlds, integrating a built environment within in-situ features. Eventually, an architect's enduring vision of a living, habitable Space may become reality.

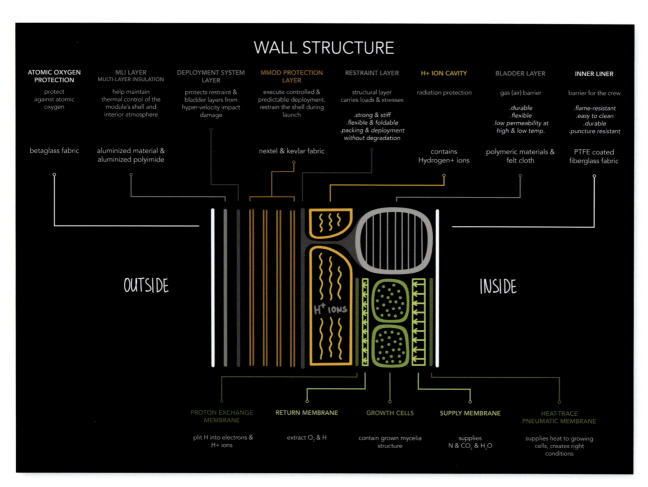

Margaryta Kaliberda and Ludovica
Breitfeld with Mahsa Abdi, Sara Laila,
Fatehmeh Mohammadi and Shada Salloum,
Mother Fungus,
Lunar Oasis Design Studio,
Research Unit Building Construction and
Design 2 (HB2), TU Wien and Abu Dhabi
University,
Vienna, Austria
2022

above: The innovative layering concept for the lunar base Mother Fungus incorporates living tissues and materials on a structural level, utilising fungi to enhance radiation protection within the habitat.

Sandra Häuplik-Meusburger,
Lunarbase Moonwalker,
'A Room with A View' exhibition,
Technical Museum Vienna (TMW),
TU Wien,
Vienna, Austria,
2023

right: The Lunarbase Moonwalker blurs boundaries between living and non-living elements through the convergence of traditional building structures, living tissue organisms and new technologies. In this symbiosis, structures can possess qualities of feeling, growth and change.

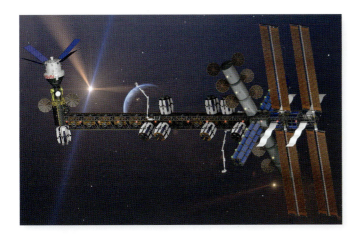

Paolo Mangili,
'Lagrange Systems for Common
Operations & Management' (LaSCOM),
Space Architecture Master's thesis project,
Sasakawa International Center
for Space Architecture (SICSA),
University of Houston,
Texas,
2023

Space architecture enables the design of space systems for habitation and the support of space science and exploration beyond low Earth orbit where each element and stage of development is conceived to allow sustainable growth for the future.

Space architects in the posthuman era will need to identify and utilise cutting-edge technologies that can meet the evolving demands. With humans moving from planet to planet and further into Space, the concept of habitability itself will be redefined by the new conditions, established goals and timelines.

Thriving will only be possible through following the path of coexisting in exploring, living and designing. Space architects who will design in and for the posthuman era should aim for deepening humanity both on Earth and in the vastness of Space.

Whatever the future holds for humanity, space architects create new design strategies that integrate learning from the past and present, teaching and sharing experiences and designing with a view to stimulating the desire to thrive and explore. Such transitions in design focus raise the question of whether the design approach for Space will evolve from a human-centred perspective to one that considers humans as one element among many other factors. Consequently, space architecture and design for supporting space exploration and future space economies should help humanity to shift away from the idea of 'colonisation' and instead embrace the unique opportunities present at any destination in Space.

Posthuman Evolution of Space Architecture

Successful coexisting design practices can help humans to maintain their humanity even in a posthuman era through understanding that being a posthuman does not require rejecting 'humanness'. Employing such design approaches compels space architects to welcome new design challenges, particularly in unfamiliar environments where humans are newcomers. It is up to humans whether to behave as isolated individuals or as respectful visitors, taking full responsibility for the legacy of what they leave behind.

The posthuman era, whether it includes different forms of humans or no humans at all, will be a result of human evolution. Nonetheless, as humans, space architects ought to consider creating a design path that does not aim for a specific destination but rather seeks to discover a path of thoughtful and sensible action. This responsibility transcends boundaries, encompassing the urgent needs of Earth and Space. ⌀

Sasakawa International Center
for Space Architecture (SICSA)
MS-Space Architecture students
researching design aspects and
habitability requirements in NASA's
Lyndon B Johnson Space Center,
Houston, Texas,
2020

Future space architects dreaming about the future while learning about the current state of the industry and architectural practices.

Text © 2024 John Wiley & Sons Ltd. Images: pp 94–5 ©TU Wien, HB2, Miruna Vecerdi and Rudolf Neumerkel; p 96(l) ©TU Wien, HB2 & ITI, Sandra Häuplik-Meusburger; pp 96(r), 97, 99 © Olga Bannova, SICSA, University of Houston; p 98(t) ©TU Wien, HB2, Margaryta Kaliberda and Ludovica Breitfeld; p 98(b) ©Technisches Museum Wien, Sandra Häuplik-Meusburger, 2023

Xavier De Kestelier,
Levent Ozruh and
Jonathan Irawan

Hassell,
ESA Lunar Habitat Framework,
South Pole,
the Moon,
2023

Interior spaces with recycled material: 3D-printed chairs and intravenous therapy (IV) bags used as alcohol bottles for a lunar bar. The project tries to find the middle ground between Earth-like cosiness and lunar material availability.

Scaling Lunar Habitats from Research Outposts to Thriving Villages

The development of liveable and fulfilling human habitats in Space is one of the current preoccupations of space architects. Their designs should be highly adaptable, reconfigurable and able to securely accommodate various functional requirements as well as multiple scales of inhabitants and operations. Multidisciplinary design practice Hassell has developed a Lunar Habitat Framework project for the European Space Agency with just these goals. Architect and Head of Design Xavier De Kestelier, architectural designer and space architect Levent Ozruh and Computational Design Lead Jonathan Irawan describe Hassell's work in this area.

The new space era centres on the human need for the means to live fulfilling lives in outer space. To address the challenges of this environment, a long-term vision is necessary, incorporating a high degree of optionality in habitation systems, infrastructure and growth. Departing from the scattershot copy-paste approach common in recent precedents for scalable lunar habitats, Hassell developed a Lunar Habitat Framework project for the European Space Agency (ESA) within its Open Space Innovation Platform (OSIP). Hassell has benefited from the regular feedback provided by ESA supervisors during the framework's two-year research and development, resulting in a system within which a wide range of modules and functions can coexist, to enable an organic and adaptive expansion of a six-person lunar research outpost into a 144-person lunar village and spaceport docking station for deep space exploration.

Hassell began the project by examining the distinct planning rules of familiar cities like New York and Barcelona, and found additional inspiration in multilevel urban circulation systems such as skywalks and underground pedestrian roads in Minneapolis, Minnesota in the US, and Toronto, Ontario in Canada. The extracted design principles inform the project, which accommodates a fully enclosed network of multilayered human circulation that ensures seamless accessibility for rovers to reach each habitat cluster.

A study conducted in partnership with Cranfield University determined that the optimal site for the framework is the lunar south pole region, specifically Cluster 1 (Connecting Ridge, C1-0 and Connecting Ridge, C1-1) near the Shackleton Crater.[1] The selection is based on factors including illumination, topography, and resource-mining potential, including ice. The chosen site also provides exposure to continuous lateral direct sunlight. In terms of materials, the framework is designed as a hybrid of prefabricated and in-situ resource utilisation (ISRU) manufactured structures – two categories belonging to A Smith's classification of lunar base structures.[2]

A scalable framework, the project is situated near the Shackleton Crater at the lunar south pole.

Scalable Growth

Allowing various organisations – space agencies, private companies and tourism – to coexist and shape the habitat neighbourhoods will facilitate the organic evolution of lunar communities. The habitat's growth will involve negotiation between the centralisation and decentralisation of programmatic functions, and fit-out changes as certain habitation modules adapt to new phases. In this process, over time some functions will be consolidated and housed in fewer, larger habitats, while others will be replicated as smaller, more numerous entities across different locations within the settlement. Each group of habitation modules is surrounded by a radiation protection shell, and the framework expands on a cluster-by-cluster basis. Thus, each growth phase will minimise the number of radiation-protection shells required. This system also optimises the multilevel circulation layers that facilitate uninterrupted human mobility. At the intersection points of the grid parcels, connector modules are vertically stacked to link all the levels, creating towers equipped with vertical arrays of solar panels on top. The lower-ground level accommodates slower movement, requiring passage through the habitation modules. This circulation system consistently connects adjacent habitats with a connector module at the centre of each cluster, minimising the number of doors required for each habitat. It also establishes multiple circulation loops, and more backup routes in case of emergencies when compared to a linear arrangement of habitats. Externally, at ground level, rover routes follow the outlines of the main grid, providing democratic access to each parcel of the framework. In contrast, the upper-ground level features express highways between the towers, enabling faster, shuttle-like circulation between key centres of the habitat.

A Kit of Parts

The habitat framework adopts modularity at various scales, incorporating a 'kit of parts' approach, from material assembly to module combinations with varying functions: radiation-protection shell, habitation module, connector modules, intersection modules and solar arrays. This not only provides a high degree of optionality within the current framework but, as a 3D multilayered system that works on the vertices of a grid rather than grid cells, it also creates further possibilities for future designs.

Radiation protection is a crucial aspect of lunar habitats. Departing from traditional 3D-printing methods, Hassell's design considers long-term scalability, sustainability and maintenance. An aggregation-based method is explored to allow for individual pieces to be added via ballistic measures or removed when needed. In other words, local changes have a lesser impact overall compared to continuous 3D printing or high-precision parts assembly. By utilising singularity in building blocks and low-precision assembly, the construction system enables long-term flexibility, repairability and redundancy. The protective shell design incorporates a temporary inflatable formwork, resulting in a central dome shape that expands into an X shape through the construction of four legs. This design approach ensures a structure that diverges from continuous, high-precision approaches that are fragile to unplanned changes. In contrast, the design explores structural anti-fragility – a term coined by the essayist and mathematical statistician Nassem Nicholas Taleb for systems that benefit from disorder.[3] Randomness becomes advantageous to aggregate interlocking. Beyond the main framework area, blaster shields around landing pads will contain dust created during landing. This potentially severe issue is also addressed by the introduction of 'suit ports' as a means of entry to the habitat, instead of traditional airlocks; this way, the suits are always left outside, attached to the building.

The radiation-protection shell encloses either a combination of four pill-shaped habitation modules or a large central habitation module. These designs are derived from careful study of human proportions and needs to

provide comfort, convenience and a flexible configuration of living spaces. As the shell design repeats across the framework for each cluster – sometimes solely as a dome structure without its four legs – the habitation modules beneath them can be combined in various ways. Similarly, the interior fit-out for each habitat can be extensively reconfigured to accommodate different functions.

The tensairity systems, developed by Airlight Ltd (now called Tensairity Solutions), and research into shell and spatial structures by Belgian architectural engineer and professor Lars De Laet, provide significant inspiration for the structural system supporting habitable pods.[4] These lightweight inflatable structures function as air beams, separating tension and compression with the volume they create. This enhances loadbearing capacity and achieves long spans, assisted by the considerably weaker lunar gravity. The foldable truss system combines hinged stiff elements with an inflatable membrane, fulfilling functional requirements and providing a natural pressure vessel shape that optimises structural integrity by distributing stress and pressure evenly. Pill-shaped modules come in two lengths, enabling versatility and the potential for increased occupancy, and incorporate an interior fit-out strategy. Modular units can be designed for research and custom equipment, with allocated space in International Standard Payload Rack (ISPR) units such as the mid-deck locker equivalent (MDLE). Inflatable drop-stitch panels provide spatial partitions, while the raised floor accommodates services. Modular wall panels offer privacy, and the embedded ceiling contains service distribution systems. Overall, the interior design seeks a balance between high sensitivity to the available material cycles of the lunar context, repurposing of items – such as the intravenous therapy (IV) bags used at the bar to store drinks – and an affordable degree of Earth materials to create a connection with home.

Modularity and advanced materiality are a key focus in the interior fit-outs, with drop-stitch panels occupying the internal surfaces of an advanced tensairity structure.

Connectivity between different habitation module types is achieved through the connector module. This module is designed to be narrow while accommodating bidirectional circulation, with an optimised form to save space for payloads. Additionally, the connector module can incorporate additional storage functions, using the excess space within the internal pressurised volume. It is also a key element of the express highway circulation system which spans the horizontal arrays between the vertical stacks of intersection modules. Due to Moon's low gravity, large spans can connect distant points in the framework, offering more efficient passage for the inhabitants.

The habitat framework accommodates a multilayered circulation system that allows maximum reach, high redundancy and rapid movement.

Vertical arrays of solar panels create structures above the habitat to maximise solar harnessing. The structures rotate to follow the Sun's position as it changes on the Moon's horizon in a 27.3-day cycle.

Aerial view of the habitat, showing the multilayered circulation systems with a porous grid that allows rover access throughout a given masterplan configuration.

Solar arrays, positioned vertically on top of towers created by the intersection modules, play a crucial role in energy distribution within the framework. Initially folded for transport, the compact structures can unfold to reveal multiple solar panels. Each solar array structure supplies sufficient energy to four neighbouring habitat clusters, ensuring decentralised energy distribution. In case of malfunction, clusters can rely on adjacent solar array structures for power. Given the project's location on the lunar south pole, the sun is always at the horizon but rotates due to the Moon's revolution around Earth. The structures follow this movement to maximise harnessed solar energy. This also creates constant exposure to sunlight, creating a 24-hour day which adversely affects the human circadian rhythm. If required, the express circulation system allows different parties to have their own diurnal cycles of light and dark without affecting each other.

Designing for the Expansion of Human Outreach

The proposed framework for lunar habitats signifies a paradigm shift in thinking about habitation beyond Earth, supporting humanity's future potential as a space-faring species and redefining what it means to be human, as well as expanding humanity's capabilities. By prioritising sustainable material cycles, wellbeing and adaptability, the project lays the foundation for a long-term human presence on the Moon – a harsh environment that will introduce new ways of living and adaptation through the expansion of human design capabilities. From a construction standpoint, the project augments the traditional understanding of human control of the environment by computing randomness to enhance structural performance. Overall, the lunar context has created new opportunities and challenges for architectural design. Low gravity enables greater spans, while strong radiation and rough terrains have driven the construction method to be based on aggregation. This scalable framework not only addresses the immediate challenges of radiation protection and connectivity, but also allows for future expansion and evolution with its modular components. ⌂

Low gravity enables greater spans, while strong radiation and rough terrains have driven the construction method to be based on aggregation

Notes

1. Philipp Gläser et al, *Illumination Conditions at the Lunar South Pole Using High-Resolution Digital Terrain Models from LOLA*, Thames & Hudson (London), 3rd edn, 2014, pp 78–90.
2. A Smith, 'Mechanics of Materials in Lunar Base Design', *Applied Mechanics Reviews* 46 (6), 1993, pp 268–71.
3. Nicholas Nassim Taleb, *Antifragile: Things That Gain from Disorder*, Penguin (London), 2013.
4. Anna Suñol, Dean Vucinic and Lars De Laet, 'Tensairity Concept Applied to Lighter-Than-Air Vehicles for Light-weight Structures', in *Proceedings of the ASME 2014 International Mechanical Engineering Congress and Exposition, Volume 1: Advances in Aerospace Technology*, ASME (Montreal), 14–20 November 2014: https://asmedigitalcollection.asme.org/IMECE/proceedings-abstract/IMECE2014/V001T01A038/261246.

Text © 2024 John Wiley & Sons Ltd. Images © Hassell

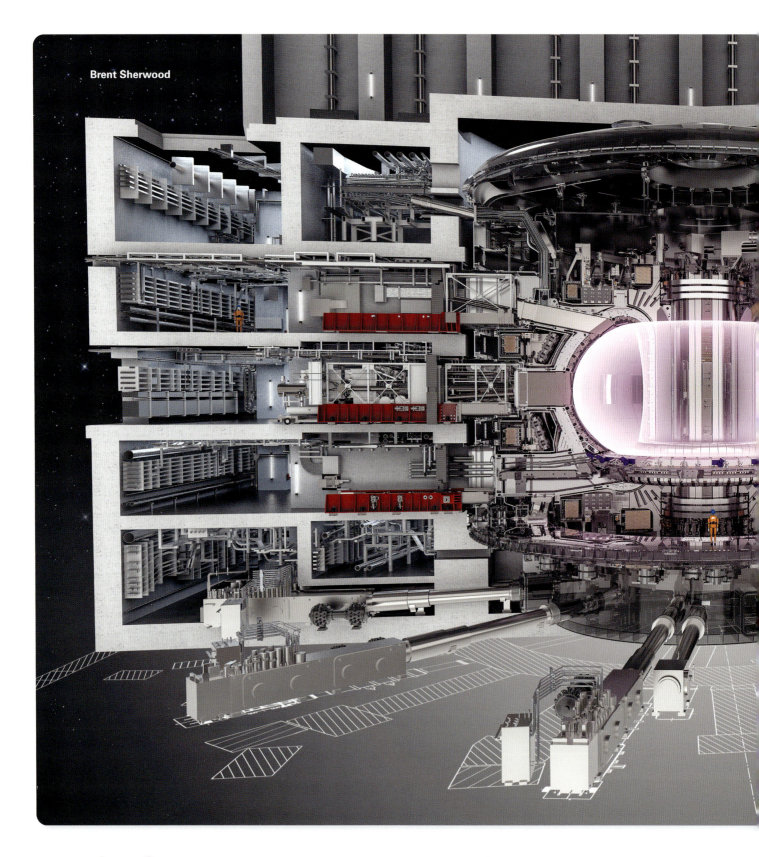

Brent Sherwood

POSTHUMAN SPACE ARCHITECTURE

MACHINE WORLDS TO SEED SPACE

Human beings are adapted to dry land and standard atmosphere, and to investigate other areas of the globe such as the sea and the air, let alone Space, we need the multivalent support of numerous machine interventions. Space architect **Brent Sherwood** explains the huge problems that must be overcome to satisfy our longing to explore extraterrestrial worlds and become truly posthuman as we travel and live beyond the confines of our planet.

Space architecture is the 'theory and practice of designing and building human environments [for use] in outer space'.[1] This emergent field – which at present concerns itself with designing small spaceships within which humans can survive, eat, sleep, work, play and voyage – tries hard to be human-centric.

But how humanised can it ever really be? The environments of outer space transcend humanity's entire experience in our native biosphere. This discontinuity impels us to explore posthuman architecture in Space: machine worlds, eco-worlds and transhuman worlds.

Earth's biosphere is a layer about half a per cent of the planet's radius, like the skin of an onion. Every other place in the accessible universe is lethal to humans. In a vacuum, without a sophisticated, hermetic envelope of reliable technology, we can only survive for seconds. Within a pressurised vessel, without strict control of temperature and atmospheric conditions, just minutes. We can survive only a few days without water, weeks without food or radiation shielding, and months without weight. In Space, all these fundamentals of life must be provided artificially, and there is perpetual risk of technical systems failure. The ultimate 'low probability, high consequence' event – impact from space debris moving 15 times faster than a bullet – adds uncertainty to every moment. And lunar and Mars dust are both toxic.

Apart from these outright risks, there is privation. To date, the tiny, hermetic bubbles of habitability shot into Space have been cramped, noisy and smelly. Air is constantly circulated to prevent asphyxiating carbon dioxide pockets, so there is no stillness. Nothing stays put unless it is fastened down. Cooking is an undeveloped technology and fresh food is rare. Zero-gravity toilets are finicky.

These inimical conditions provoke a key question: 'Then why in the world … ?' Four answers are: novel experiences bringing new perspectives; endless horizons to explore; inexhaustible resources, and limitless human expansion.[2] Space has the resources; and capacity to unlock an unlimited future for civilisation, and one of the keys to the lock is architecture that can sustain humans in inherently uninhabitable places, indefinitely.

VFR Consortium,
ITER Tokamak Complex,
Cadarache, France,
2025–35

previous pages: A fusion power test facility is designed around the containment of unimaginable energies. Our world is already based on architecture for machines doing machine things.

NEOM,
The Line,
Saudi Arabia,
2022–

The Line will be a megacity-scale 'machine for living in'. The essential infrastructure for power production, water desalination and waste treatment are not evident.

Brent Sherwood, Makoto Eyre and Jeffrey Montes, Orbital Reef Core Module, Low Earth orbit, 2028

The Orbital Reef space station is space architecture for the 2030s. Essential infrastructure is adjacent, making continuously apparent what it takes to sustain human living.

Living in the Machine

In 1923, Le Corbusier famously declared 'a house is a machine for living in', reflecting the first century of Industrial Age modernisation.[3] A hundred years later, today's networked environments, condition-responsive building envelopes, digital windows, plumbing that monitors epidemiology, transformable structures, remote control and machine intelligence have made modern houses into actual machines.

Cities, too, have evolved into 'machines for civilisation'. Omnipresent Wi-Fi, mass transit, networked traffic control, ubiquitous surveillance, smart utilities and continuous renovation of the built fabric amplify the complex interactions that have always characterised urban density. By evolving ways of making humans more efficient, houses and cities increasingly take on the attributes of posthuman machines.

Machines for living in Space are yet more posthuman. As in naval architecture, spacefarers live and work inside machinery that is dominated by nonhuman functions. We can hide the machinery from the occupants, camouflaging its geometry and absorbing its sound and vibrations, but it is machine architecture nonetheless. In Space however, the surrounding natural environment is quickly lethal; lacking a survivable outdoors, we can only contrive artificial 'outside' environments that simulate life in the open. Behind the bulkheads, between the decks and surrounding the whole exterior, the machine must run without fail.

The International Space Station sets a sobering benchmark. Humans live at the heart of this posthuman architecture for a single purpose: laboratory research. It takes 450 tonnes of equipment, with acreage as big as a football field, powering an environment approximately the size of the interior of a Boeing 777 airliner, to support half a dozen humans. A spaceship designed to take half a dozen people to Mars and back on a three-year voyage – a very different goal – retains the same ratio of technology to payload: a few precious humans ensconced within massive infrastructure including propellants, power- and life-support equipment, electronics and shielding.

Architecture for Machines

Most of the built environment humanity will use to expand out into the solar system will not even be intended for humans. Powering Earth from Space, and making the stuff of space civilisation out of lunar dirt, will require vast machinery. Only the strength, finesse, scale, ceaseless work capacity and productivity of robots can handle the hazards and remoteness. Such a machine world, populated by machines doing machine things, is fundamentally posthuman. Humans will only episodically intercede. It will not be quite the vividly posthuman terror of the assimilated human Locutus at the heart of an alien Borg cube, but it begins to feel that way. The challenges of Space make space civilisation unavoidably posthuman.

Yet, even on Earth, posthuman architecture is already here. We already build machine worlds that accommodate humans only at the margins. Architecture for energy production, material handling, manufacturing, transportation and information processing dominate our total built environment. Power plants, factories, transportation hubs, fulfillment centres and server farms are designed for machines. Humans are only one of the seven users of airports (the others are aircraft, service vehicles, ground transit, baggage, freight and retail goods). Human users do not think much about the other six, but architects must. We tend to zone our machine and inhabited worlds apart, but large swaths of Earth are becoming like Trantor, the fictional galactic capital of Asimov's *Foundation* series: a planet entirely wrapped in construction. Space architecture merely makes the reality evident.

Eventually, perhaps, vessels for years-long interplanetary or even interstellar voyages might use hibernation to keep the crew healthy. Posthuman architecture, devoid of motion or change, would then support life suspended, quiet except for the susurration of machines.

The need for the posthuman becomes even clearer when we regard food production. Locally produced food will be essential for living in Space. On Earth, agriculture does not often drive architecture, but in Space, every cubic metre must be constructed and climate-controlled

John Mankins,
Solar Power Satellite ALPHA,
geosynchronous Earth orbit,
2040s

A kilometre (0.6 mile) across, each SPS ALPHA power transmission station could supplant one terrestrial 1-GW nuclear or coal-fired power plant. Space industry's machine architecture is posthuman in requirements, type and scale.

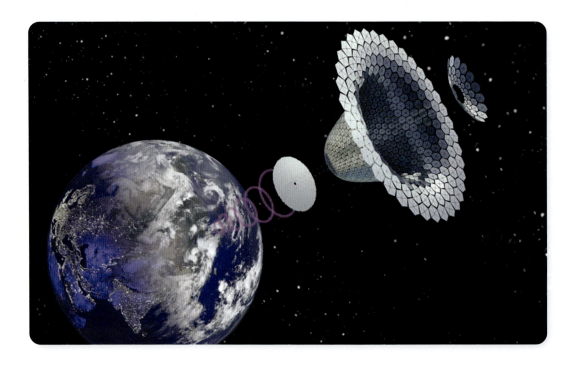

European Space Agency (ESA), Micro-Ecological Life Support System Alternative (MELiSSA) project, Barcelona, 2009

The developmental facility uses plants as part of machinery to purify air and water for four humans. Complex technology allows compactness.

Space Architecture for Nonhuman Life

Environments for nonhuman life forms are a second type of posthuman space architecture. The International Space Station keeps its half-dozen people alive with multiple racks of complex equipment: redundant pumps, tubes, filters, reactant beds, ducts, fans, sensors and processors. But this is not scalable. Somewhere along the path from dozens of spacefarers in the 2030s to hundreds by mid-century (say, in an orbital resort), to thousands in a future settlement, our life-support technology must shift from 'physicochemical' to biological.

That is how Earth's environment functions: the water cycle distils salt water into fresh, microbes purify groundwater, and forests and ocean plankton metabolise carbon dioxide for photosynthesis and produce oxygen as a by-product. The roadmap to biological life support begins with hybrid systems that incorporate microbes and plants into densified, highly engineered eco-loops. Today's experiments require complex machinery and constant maintenance – architecturally, they are not much different from the physicochemical state of practice. The smaller the scale, the more complex the technology.

Earth's biosphere buffer is vast and unimaginably complex, and barely understood. We do not yet know how to balance the size and complexity necessary to sustain artificial eco-worlds. In the early 1990s in Oracle, Arizona, the Biosphere 2 experiment enclosed people in what was hoped would be a hermetic self-sustaining ecosystem. It demonstrated just how important a large buffer is for 'closed ecological life support'. One hectare of complex biomes, contained in a 180,000-cubic-metre (6.36 million-cubic-foot) habitat 13 orders of magnitude smaller than Earth's own 'Biosphere 1', was unable to sustain just eight humans for two years.

Yet Biosphere 2 points towards an important type of space architecture: a vast vivarium. Mastering the principles of closure – buffer, balance, diversity and intervention – will let us sustain multi-species ecosystems indefinitely. Using space resources, we can then manufacture unlimited eco-worlds in Space to settle the solar system.

No one has yet demonstrated how to make a huge pressure vessel in Space. Containing atmospheric pressure at a large scale creates enormous tensile loads, which are compounded by the weight produced by rotation for artificial gravity. However, physicist Gerard K O'Neill and his space colonisation study teams at Princeton University and NASA showed in the mid-1970s that suspension-bridge structure systems with even prosaic material properties can enable kilometre-scale interiors.[4] This is how eco-worlds could be built, so we must become proficient at it.

Ironically, however, Earth-like eco-worlds will be posthuman, too. Their size, layout and systems for controlling atmosphere, temperature, water and recycling must be optimised for nonhuman life forms.

Here, a pattern is revealed: humans are but a tiny component of both machine worlds and eco-worlds. Space is uninhabitable, and offers nothing ready-made for human use. When 'externalities' simply do not exist, cognisance of the ratio of posthuman stuff to people becomes inescapable. An honest accounting of what it takes to sustain a single modern human life – let alone a community embedded in a complex ecosystem – is a gift of awareness that space architecture can bring to decision-making on Earth today.

The need for the posthuman becomes even clearer when we regard food production. Locally produced food will be essential for living in Space. On Earth, agriculture does not often drive architecture, but in Space, every cubic metre must be constructed and climate-controlled, and every litre of water and kilogramme of nutrients must be accounted for. The most optimistic estimates for a vegetarian subsistence diet require about 20 square metres (210 square feet) of intensively gardened plant-growing surface per person. Developmental experiments for space farming favour hybrids with low water demand, low growing volume, high yield and low bio-waste.

Sowing, tending, harvesting and processing will need to be robotic. Integration with everyday human activities is impractical. Concepts for large-scale space settlements have always recognised that space architecture for agriculture should be segregated, optimised for plants and machines rather than humans. Designs for high-yield environments favor a CO_2-enriched atmosphere that is toxic to humans. Spectrum-efficient grow-lighting (lacking green wavelengths, and thus inhumanly purplish) and highly automated, robotically operated, densely packed hydroponic growing systems will characterise factory farms for Space.

Eco-worlds are not simply posthuman architecture, they are post-Earth habitats. Even when we can make and manage eco-worlds, what will we have created? Scale certainly matters. A wild adult cougar needs over 125 square kilometres of range even with abundant prey. We can put 'charismatic' large animals in an O'Neill colony, but manufactured eco-worlds can never be more than zoological parks. We cannot bridge the 13 orders of magnitude that separate Biosphere 2 from Biosphere 1, nor can we design artificial homes to host all the richness of Earth life. Space architecture cannot be Noah's ark. Can appreciating this limitation also gift us with the awareness to make us better stewards of Biosphere 1?

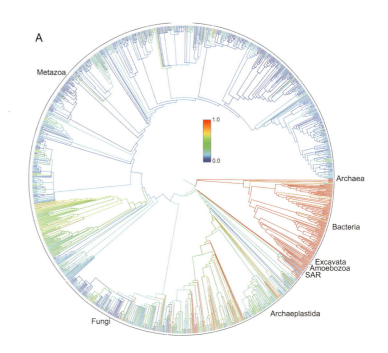

```
Blue Origin,
O'Neill Cylinder concept,
Earth-distance heliocentric orbit,
2018
```

Even enormous eco-worlds will require constant management due to their limited volume. Such small scales are curated parks, not wilderness.

```
Opentreeoflife.org,
Tree of life,
2015
```

above: Every branch in this image of the tree has at least 500 species. The complexity of Earth's biosphere is too vast to be contained in manufactured eco-worlds. Earth is irreplaceable.

Liquifer Systems Group, EDEN ISS, Antarctica (2015–19) and the Moon (2030s)

The project combines human and posthuman environments. Transhuman evolution enabled by designer biology will eventually overtake the need for hamster-tube space architecture.

Architecture for Transhumans

We can build tiny bubbles of machine architecture, partition them from Earth's biosphere, take them into the hostile environments of Space, and aggregate them into warrens for humankind. Traditional technology – materials, systems, energy and information – can make outer space habitable, but only barely.

In the future, we will use biotechnology to directly tackle the hostile environments of Space. Theoretical physicist Freeman Dyson suggested in 1985 that the most realistic scenario for inhabiting the cosmos would be to redesign organisms to suit Space conditions.[5] Rather than keeping the environment out by shielding Earth life inside Earth-like bubbles, we should design cells that self-repair radiation damage, tissues that tolerate low pressure and extreme temperatures, organ functions that do not require Earth gravity signals and plants that photosynthesise starlight.

Dyson was extrapolating, but biology is chemistry and chemistry is physics. Today we already have gene therapy and cloned pets, and medical intervention nanodevices are at hand. It is unreasonable to predict a near-limitless future for humans, animals, plants and microbes in Space by assuming unchanging biological systems within protective bubbles. By sharing the habitability burden between technology and biology, we will adapt to harsh conditions.

Multi-generation interstellar travel also requires avoiding 'genetic bottlenecks' in cosmically dispersed small populations. Managing genetic diversity uses the same transhuman biotechnology as remaking biology to suit Space. Our transhuman progeny will settle the cosmos.

What will transhuman space architecture even be? When functions traditionally performed by technology become intrinsic to our being, what sort of architecture will we need? As our very nature evolves, our built environment then becomes posthuman in the purest sense.

Posthuman Architecture Opens the Universe

Designers live to design. The allure of space architecture for architects has always been the need and opportunity to reinvent every aspect of the built environment, from utensils and furniture, to enclosure and infrastructure. When the native environment is lethal and even gravity is a parameter, everything needs to be rethought – a heady motivator for designers. Space architecture has a posthuman essence. Today, we make machines for living in, and we make architecture for machines. Tomorrow, we will design self-sustaining, independent eco-worlds. And someday, we will redesign life itself to fit the conditions of infinite Space. ᗞ

Notes
1. Team Eleven, 'The Millennium Charter: Fundamental Principles of Space Architecture', 12 October 2002: http://spacearchitect.org/wp-content/uploads/2020/06/The-Millennium-Charter.pdf.
2. Brent Sherwood, 'Comparing Future Options for Human Space Flight', *Acta Astronautica* 69, 2011, pp 346–53.
3. Le Corbusier, *Vers Une Architecture* [1923], tr Frederick Etchells as *Towards a New Architecture*, J Rodker (London), 1931, reprint Dover Publications (New York), 1985.
4. Gerard K O'Neill, *The High Frontier: Human Colonies in Space*, William Morrow & Co (New York), 1976.
5. Freeman Dyson, *Infinite in All Directions: Gifford Lectures Given at Aberdeen, Scotland, April–November 1985*, Harper & Row (New York), 1988.

Text © 2024 John Wiley & Sons Ltd. Images: pp 110–11 © ITER Organization; p 112 © NEOM; pp 113, 116(b) © Blue Origin; p 114 © John Mankins, Artemis Innovation Management Solutions, LLC; p 115 © MELiSSA Foundation; p 116(t) E Cody Hinchliff *et al*, 'Synthesis of Phylogeny and Taxonomy into a Comprehensive Tree of Life', *Proceedings of the National Academy of Sciences* 112 (41), 2015, pp 12,764–12,769. Copyright Hinchliff *et al*; p 117 © EDEN ISS consortium, visualisation: LIQUIFER

Mark Garcia

21ST–CENTURY POSTHUMAN SPACESHIP AND SPACECRAFT ARCHITECTURES

Alberto Fernández González and Mark Garcia,
Starship Interiors no 587219,
2023

An artificial-intelligence (AI) response to textual and image prompts curated by Mark Garcia exploring the aesthetics, forms, styles, geometries, topologies and morphologies of the design and technologies of the interiors of far-future posthuman starships.

Guest-Editor **Mark Garcia** takes us on a spatial journey through some of the notions and precedents of spaceships and spacecraft, their fictive and architectural precursors and current conceptual preoccupations. The contexts these new posthuman architectures and posthumans will have to occupy, endure and travel through are mind-boggling in their varied complexity.

Not all posthumanisms are equally posthuman or posthumanising. One candidate for most-posthuman architecture is the spacecraft or spaceship, which is simultaneously the 21st century's most significant and innovative architecture. This is because a unique set of new posthuman elements, technologies, contexts and agencies have coupled themselves to spaceships/spacecraft to generate the first forms of 'astro posthuman' architectures. 21st-century spaceships/spacecraft are extending the time, mix and range of species and technologies into microgravity- and gravity-modulated spaces. These temporarily or permanently change human bodies and brains (each species is impacted differently). More planetary posthuman spaces and now post-planetary spaceships/spacecraft (space stations, orbitals etc) are being designed and built than ever before, and they are increasingly culturally visible. For some posthuman theorists these astro-posthuman forces are (or will be) speciating humans and other agents and assemblages into a new astro-posthuman subject. Autobiographical accounts of astronauts who have stayed at the International Space Station (ISS) confirm this empirically, in their different ways.

The major sub-typologies of spaceships and spacecraft include probes, fly-bys, orbiters, landers, penetrators, satellites, observatories, telescopes, constellations, spacestations, interstellar and multigenerational space-arks, worldships, starships and even artificial or propulsively augmented cities and planets. The specific astro-posthuman profiles (properties, features, dimensions, technologies, elements, qualities) and their posthuman effects differ in their major taxa – between terrestrial and alien, manned and unmanned, parent and offspring/sibling craft, habitable or nonhabitable, single-manned or more (the spacesuit is a one-person spacecraft) – and through a range of programmatic/functional, mission-type, destination-type, technology-based, gravity-modified or micro-gravitational, fractionated/constellation or single-unit and even life-containing/life-supporting types. As a whole, this intersectional matrix and multiplicity of spaceships and spacecraft can also be understood as a meta-planetary space-architecture infrastructural system/network with a relatively homologous vernacular techno-aesthetics, a hyper-object ranging across the full electromagnetic spectrum of all architecture, both real and including the 'spectacular posthumanisms'[1] of mass-transmedia, universe-building gesamtkunstwerks of fictional spaceships such as those from *Star Trek* (the international iconic sci-fi screen media franchise that began in the US with a 1966 television series and became an ongoing cultural phenomenon).

SpaceX,
Starships under construction,
Boca Chica, Texas,
2023

Starship is the planned manned spacecraft of longest return flight to date. With a flexible architecture adaptable for taking humans to and landing directly on the Moon and then on to Mars, it is required to undertake planetary launch and atmospheric entry/re-entry and must therefore be 'astrodynamic' in form, structure and style.

Astro-Posthuman Theories and Concepts
Key posthuman concepts that define astro-posthuman technologies, elements, features and qualities and those that apply to identifying posthuman aspects (indexing mostly technologies, media and organisms) of spaceships and spacecraft include: a-human, artificial intelligence (AI), algorithms, algorithmic studies, alienation, altergorithms, animacies, biological arts, the computational turn, cosmo-politics, critical posthumanism, digital philosophy, ecologies of architecture, eco-materialism, eco-sophy, epigenetic landscapes, extended cognition, genetic engineering, inter-mediality, materialist informatics, media-natures, meta-modernism, multispecies relations, nature-cultures, neo-cybernetics, new materialisms, nomadic sensibility, nonhuman agency, organoids, planetarity, post-animalism, posthuman literature and criticism, post-images, resilience, robo-philosophy, speculative posthumanism, survival symbiogenesis, technicity, techno-animalism, transcorporeality and transhumanism.

Whilst some of the most eminent space and posthuman theorists and philosophers such as Francesca Ferrando, Michio Kaku, Robert Zubrin and Louis Friedman agree that migration to space and the futures of humanity must be posthuman,[2] they are largely silent on the astro-posthuman design of spaceships and spacecraft themselves. Only a few have commented briefly on limited aspects of the posthuman in relation, and these do not consider the ISS or the full range of United Space Ship Enterprise (USSE) versions, posthuman elements or the techno-aesthetics of these.[3] Others explicitly but only glancingly reference the posthuman in relation to spatial design and take narrow 'landscape' and 'geography' approaches to posthuman spatial design.[4]

Space archaeologist Alice Gorman has referenced spacecraft as 'satellites' and 'space-junk',[5] although of the extant books explicitly on posthuman architectures, only a couple mention space architecture examples and only cursorily.[6] The closest book-length texts which touch on posthuman spaceships and spacecraft – social scientist Konrad Szocik's *Human Enhancements for Space Missions* (2020)[7] and philosopher and ecologist Timothy Morton's *Spacecraft* (2021)[8] – do not discuss the USSE or ISS.

In his book, Szocik does not address posthuman spaceships/spacecraft aesthetics per se, though there are positive discussions of both posthumanisms in a number of its articles and one in which *Star Trek* is posited as a realistic vision for the future of space exploration.[9] Morton's book takes a flat-ontological position to spaceships, though he simultaneously focuses misguidedly on the Millennium Falcon (from *Star Wars*). But there is no literature, project or design exploring how the posthuman technologies, indicators, qualities and effects could all be fully integrated into a spacecraft or spaceship – let alone a space architecture. A fuller set of posthuman properties and potentials (or combinations of these in spaceships and spacecraft) that define astro-posthuman complexes and their techno-aesthetics need to be integrated systematically and strategically into the future design and theorisation of spaceships and spacecraft to enable their full posthuman potentials.

The two most representative, famous, extensively documented spaceships/spacecraft exemplars – the ISS (spacecraft) and USSE (spaceship) – happen also to be the most posthuman examples of each type. But despite their preeminent status in these categories, they are enormously architecturally under-theorised – in relation to the aesthetics of their technologies and the technologies of their aesthetics, as much as their unparalleled planetary effects.

USS Enterprise
There have always been many clear and well-documented causal links and effects between NASA and *Star Trek*.[10] Space scientists, astronomers and spacecraft engineers, as well as real space architects (like senior NASA architect Scott Howe, and Rachel Armstrong, Leuven University Professor of Architecture), produce science-fiction works where astro-posthumanisms are now the default spaceship design mode.[11] The most expensive, most co-designed, most transmediatised, most widely disseminated and most profit-generating spaceship is *Star Trek*'s USS Enterprise (USSE). No other work of unbuilt architecture is worth the current franchise value of US$10.6 billion. No other 'building' has been evolving (since 1966) for a comparable length of design-time and tens if not hundreds of thousands of iterations involving thousands of scientists, engineers, technologists, designers and artists, across 14 feature films and over 890 (hour-long plus) episodes of television.

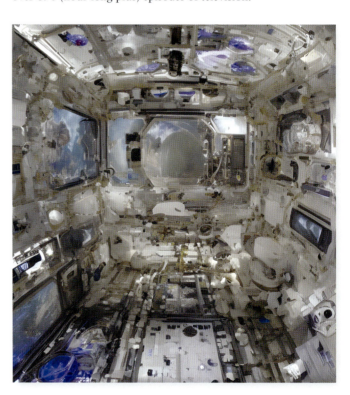

Alberto Fernández González and Mark Garcia,
Spacestation Zoo,
Synthesis no 162661,
2023

The result of the prompt 'spacestation zoo' from an artificial intelligence (AI), this image points to the non-natural, cramped state in which most nonhuman life exists on the ISS and other spacecraft. Despite a more generous-looking volume than the ISS, the space still appears inadequate as a 'zoo'. A full inventory of the plants, animals and other life forms and cells which have been in space needs to be compiled, monitored and fully analysed if the astro-posthuman is to be fully posthuman for all nonhumans.

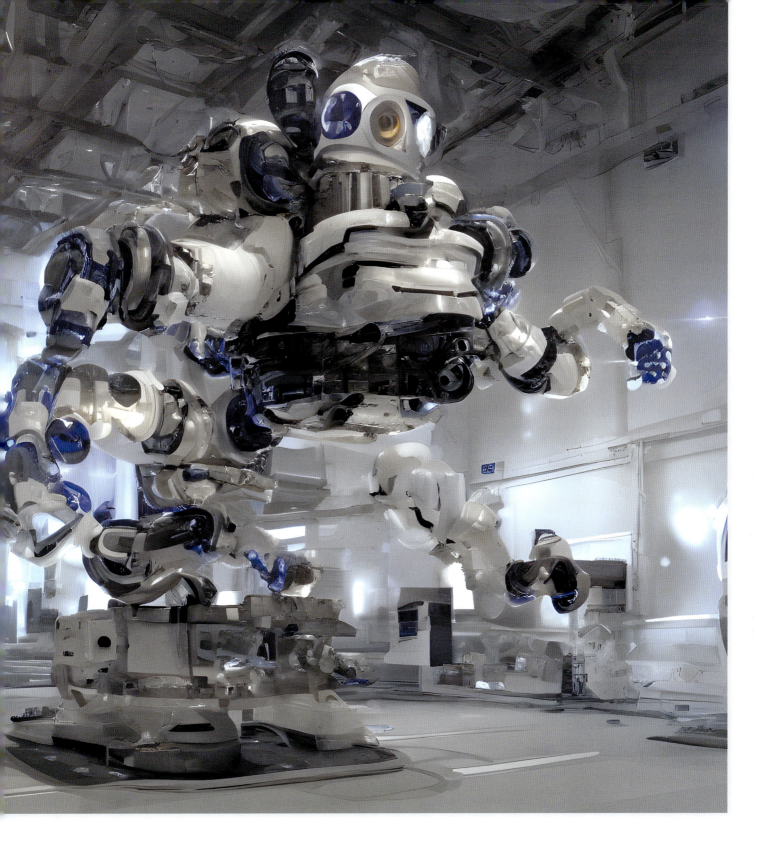

Alberto Fernández González and Mark Garcia,
Space Robotics,
Synthesis no 22673,
2023

Space robotics coupled with AI is a ubiquitous and perhaps the fastest-growing, most productive and most astro-posthumanising assemblage found in all spacecraft and spaceships. An AI response to the prompt 'space robotics' indicates the new type and scale of astro-posthuman exo-robotics that microgravity will yield in terms of form, style and aesthetics.

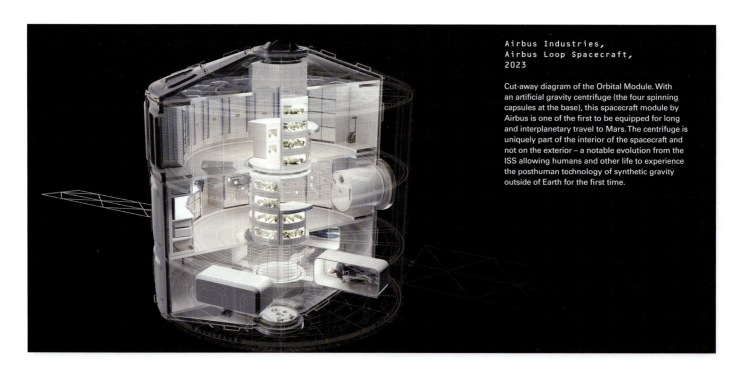

Airbus Industries,
Airbus Loop Spacecraft,
2023

Cut-away diagram of the Orbital Module. With an artificial gravity centrifuge (the four spinning capsules at the base), this spacecraft module by Airbus is one of the first to be equipped for long and interplanetary travel to Mars. The centrifuge is uniquely part of the interior of the spacecraft and not on the exterior – a notable evolution from the ISS allowing humans and other life to experience the posthuman technology of synthetic gravity outside of Earth for the first time.

The ultimate posthuman spaceship is arguably the most posthuman architecture ever imagined

Photo of the Eaglemoss Starship Nog model, 2023

In the search for new and future aesthetics, forms, styles, geometries, topologies and morphologies of the design and technologies of the interiors of present and near-future posthuman spacecraft, the universe of science-fiction architectural design can offer glimpses of the proleptic. The influence of architect Zaha Hadid is obvious.

Its multicultural saturation and influence has been global for decades and, though it has been largely ignored by architectural and interior design academics and professionals, many academics and researchers have written articles and books on the general importance of *Star Trek* to architecture and specifically the USSE's architectural design and technoaesthetics, as well as the specific value and links between *Star Trek* and science,[12] philosophy,[13] history,[14] technology[15] and art – which includes the multi-volume visual catalogue of the evolutions of USSE versions (and related volumes published by Hero Collector, London).[16] Currently appearing in an unprecedented three parallel series of *Star Trek* – namely *Discovery*, *Strange New Worlds* and *Picard* – the versions of the USSE are now and continue to become even more posthuman than ever. The ultimate posthuman spaceship is therefore arguably the most posthuman architecture ever imagined, designed and (mostly) realised. In comparison to all spacecraft, the USSE shows not only the ways in which the ISS is more successful because it is posthumanising, but how all spacecraft could become more impactful as architecture if they were more posthuman in more carefully integrated ways.

International Space Station
Costing around US$127 billion and being the product of 15–16 collaborating nations over the past 25 years, the ISS is therefore one of the most innovative, significant, multi-authored and highest innovation-producing architectural designs in history. Its research and benefits to Earth through planetary observation and imaging, water purification, meteorology, disaster early warning and mitigation and biology (predominantly astrobiology, plant and microbe research) are unprecedented and will continue to be of great benefit to all humanity[17] and some posthumanity. Whilst the most filmed, surveilled, digitised, analysed and broadcast work of 21st-century architecture, its research data and image collection, functions, technologies, economic and geopolitical value, and architectural and interior design technoaesthetics have been largely ignored. Instead, what is communicated, promoted and valued are its other science, engineering and technology transfers.

In terms of some more holistic and real-built, test case-studies of successful techno-aesthetic transfers from posthuman spaceships and spacecraft to other architectures, the most significant and recent include the NASA Sustainability Base at Ames Research Center, Moffett Field, California (2016) by William McDonough Architects. More domestic and vernacular are the capsular work of Richard Horden (such as the Micro Compact Home (2005)), and other modular, 'neo-metabolist' and 'pre-fabricated housing' such as those of the RV Prototype (2012) by Greg Lynn, Mercury Houses One and Two (2001 and 2004) and LaCoccinella (2014) by Architecture and Vision (Arturo Vittori and Andreas Vogler), and the Lunar Lander house (2013) by Kurt Hughes. More spectacular and major works are the National Space Centre in Leicester, UK (2001) by Grimshaw Architects and the NetDragon Websoft Headquarters in Fuzhou, China (2015) by Liu Dejiang which is the only *Star Trek*-related building in the world to have been officially licensed by CBS – the series' current broadcasters. Decisively, astro-posthuman spaceships and spacecraft are the only way to save anything terrestrial.

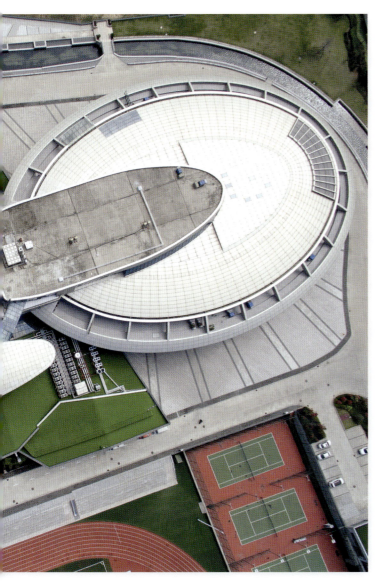

Liu Dejiang,
NetDragon Websoft Headquarters,
Fuzhou City, China,
2015

Aerial view of a real USSE. An aesthetic transfer from the fictional to a non-functioning ersatz and kitsch Postmodern (rather than posthuman) €100-million pop-pastiche of Star Trek's Starship Enterprise. The only work of architecture to have obtained a licence from broadcaster CBS to replicate the form of the USSE. The building is an office for games software designers and is as large as three football pitches. The design of the interiors is not known to be similar to the USSE.

NASA,
Render of the Lunar Gateway
with Orion Capsule,
the Moon,
2019

below: Part of the Artemis programme, the new lunar gateway is planned to launch in 2025 for missions to the Moon and as a staging post for Deep Space Transport missions to Mars. Based on modules tested on the ISS, this new spacecraft project is led by NASA in collaboration with the Canadian Space Agency, the European Space Agency and the Japanese Space Agency, as well as private-sector partners, for expeditions to the lunar south pole.

Alberto Fernández González
and Mark Garcia,
Space Film Interiors no 518243,
2023

right: An AI response to textual and image prompts curated by Mark Garcia to discover the aesthetics, forms, styles, geometries, topologies and morphologies of the design and technologies of the interiors of present and future posthuman spaceships in science-fiction films.

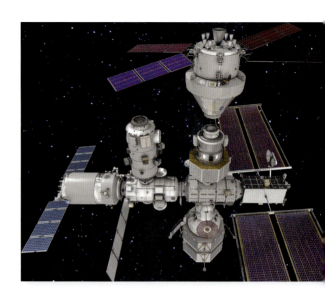

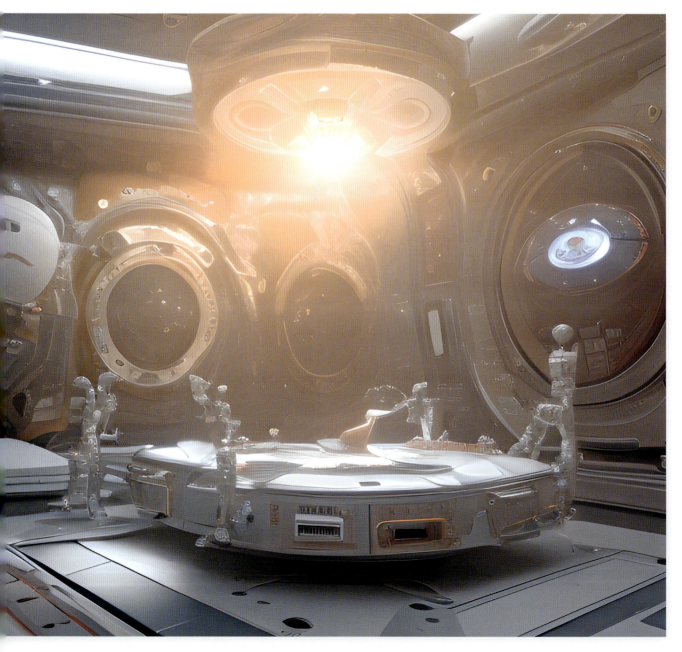

Post-21st-Century Posthuman Spaceship and Spacecraft Architectures

From 2009 to 2018 the Kepler Space Telescope discovered around 2,662 exoplanets, of which 750 were in the 'habitable zone' and may contain water – possible new planets for Earth species, which may also contain alien life and therefore perhaps xeno-architectures.[18] The year 2016 saw the first proof that gravitational waves exist – leading to a new type of gravitational telescope, the gravitational observatory – the Laser Interferometer Space Antenna (LISA) spacecraft – as much as its attendant new subdiscipline. As of 2023, the US$10 billion James Webb Space Telescope (JWST) now offers us views across 25 billion light years of space and as far back in the early universe as 13.5 billion years – simultaneously including the largest scope of imaging across the full electromagnetic spectrum. There is therefore no other more historical architecture.

And in terms of the architectural fundamental of gravity, beyond our future utilisation of the power and nature of the graviton, the JWST will shortly reveal the most detailed images of our new other centre – Sagittarius A*, first observed by NASA's Chandra spacecraft and confirmed in 2020 to be the black hole our galaxy orbits around. Gravitational observatories including that of the forthcoming LISA spacecraft will be the largest observatory and architectural structure ever: an orbiting triangle with three 2.5-million-kilometre (1.5-million-mile) laser arms. These spacecraft are discovering the architectures of the largest structures in the universe – its galactic superclusters and its largest known agent: the singularity known as the 'Great Attractor'. As far as the most fundamental, significant, innovative and multidisciplinary histories, theories and futures are concerned, spaceships and spacecraft are the most important architectures (let alone posthuman architectural) designs, ever.

Wormholes, rogue and exo-planets, silicon-based and alien life exist at the speculative edges of the teleology and value of posthuman spaceships and spacecraft architectures. But these are not just the most philosophical architectures of the fundamentals of gravity, the Earth, life, matter, our galaxy and deep universal space, histories and futures. These astro-posthuman architectures are expanding the meanings and relevance of architecture for our new posthuman era into the architecture of space itself. Contained within these posthuman architectures are also the post-history and post-futures of post-architecture. Not only will posthuman architectures and spacecraft be for posthumans; we could choose to be, in a sense, posthuman architectures (including spaceships and spacecraft) in ourselves. Posthuman spaceships and spacecraft are architectures that could make the posthuman *Homo spatiens* as much as make a possible future where humans are naturally extinct, at least on Earth. Let the posthuman spacecraft and spaceships bloom. ◊

Notes

1. Drew Ayers, *Spectacular Posthumanism: The Digital Vernacular of Digital Effects*, Bloomsbury (London), 2018.
2. Francesca Ferrando, 'Why Space Migration Must Be Posthuman', in James SJ Schwartz and Tony Milligan (eds), *The Ethics of Space Exploration*, Springer International (Cham, Switzerland), 2016, pp 137–52; Michio Kaku, *The Future of Humanity: Terraforming Mars, Interstellar Travel, Immortality, and Our Destiny Beyond Earth*, Doubleday (New York), 2018; Robert Zubrin, *The Case for Space: How the Revolution in Spaceflight Opens Up a Future of Limitless Possibility*, Prometheus (Amherst, NY), 2020; Louis Friedman, *Human Spaceflight: From Mars to the Stars*, University of Arizona Press (Tucson, AZ), 2015.
3. For example Rachel Armstrong (ed), *Star Ark: A Living, Self-Sustaining Spaceship*, Springer (New York), 2017, and Lisa Meinecke, '"Veins and Muscles of the Universe": Posthumanism and Connectivity in *Star Trek: Discovery*', in Sabrina Mittermeier and Mareike Spychala, *Fighting for the Future: Essays on 'Star Trek: Discovery'*, Liverpool University Press (Liverpool), 2023, pp 373–90.
4. See, for example, Liam Young (ed), △ *Machine Landscapes: Architectures of the Post-Anthropocene*, January/February (no 1), 2019.
5. Alice Gorman, 'Ghost in the Machine: Space Junk and the Future of Earth Orbit', in ibid, pp 106–11.
6. Peter Baofu, *The Future of Post-Human Architecture*, Cambridge International Science Publishing (Cambridge), 2012; and Jacopo Leveratto, *Posthuman Architectures: A Catalogue of Archetypes*, Apple Academic & Design (San Francisco, CA), 2021.
7. Konrad Szocik, *Human Enhancements for Space Missions*, Springer (New York), 2020.
8. Timothy Morton. *Spacecraft*, Bloomsbury (London), 2021.
9. James SJ Schwartz, 'The Accessible Universe: On the Choice to Require Bodily Modification for Space Exploration', in Szocik, op cit, pp 201–15.
10. See, for example, Constance Penley, *NASA/TREK: Popular Science and Sex in America*, Verso (New York), 1997.
11. See the references in Simone Caroti, *The Generation Starship in Science Fiction: A Critical History 1934–2001*, McFarland (Jefferson, NC), 2011 and *The Culture Series of Iain M Banks: A Critical Introduction*, McFarland (Jefferson, NC) for examples.
12. Mark Brake, *The Science of Star Trek*, Skyhorse (Brattleboro, VT), 2022.
13. Kevin S Decker and Jason T Eberl (eds), *The Ultimate Star Trek and Philosophy: The Search for Socrates*, Blackwell (Oxford), 2016.
14. Nancy R Reagin, *Star Trek and History*, John Wiley & Sons (Hoboken, NJ), 2013.
15. Mark Lasbury, *The Realization of Star Trek Technologies*, Springer (New York), 2016.
16. Ben Robinson et al, *Star Trek: Designing Starships* series, Eaglemoss (London), 2020–21.
17. Julie Robinson et al, *International Space Station: Benefits for Humanity*, 3rd edn, NASA (Houston, TX), 2018.
18. See Armen Avanessian et al, *Perhaps It Is High Time for a Xeno-architecture to Match*, Sternberg (Berlin), 2018.

Text © 2024 John Wiley & Sons Ltd. Images: pp 118–19, 122–3, 126(bl) © Alberto Fernández González and Mark Garcia, AI-generated images created using Stable Diffusion; pp 120–21 Mark A Sherman / Shutterstock; p 124(t) © Airbus Industries; p 124(b) © Mark Garcia; pp 124–5(b) © Imaginechina Limited / Alamy Stock Photo; p 126(tr) © NASA

FROM ANOTHER PERSPECTIVE

A Word from ᴀD Editor
Neil Spiller

THE ULTIMATE SIN

THE SUPER-SURREALIST BODY

A body that is no longer anatomical, but a focus of desires. An act of love which is no longer mere self-gratification or the taking possession of, but an orgy of fantasies, projections, substitutions, displacements, even hallucinations [...] as the interchange of meanings which repeat themselves infinitely in mirror image.
— Xavière Gauthier, *Surréalisme et sexualité*, 1971[1]

Scorched flesh still smouldering, flaming heads, poorly done prison-like tattoos, words carved into necks, backs, torsos, faces, grotesque bodies, paintings seemingly mocking the virtuosity of the Old Masters, sending them, perhaps, spinning in their graves, yet also exhibiting considerable artifice themselves. Contemporary artist Christian Rex van Minnen combines the aesthetically low code with the aesthetically high code. His portraiture and otherworldly still lifes seem to come from some posthuman dystopic future. A world where most inhabitants' viscerality and vascularity is still recognisable as vaguely human, but where they are often eyeless, distended, hybridised, puckered, primitively graffiti-ed and penetrated, and punctuated by multicoloured Gummy candies.

Christian Rex van Minnen,
Untitled,
2022

opposite: Some might describe Van Minnen's art as grotesque. Indeed, the grotesque collapses space, ideas and objects that are normally epistemologically separate and often judiciously kept apart.

Beautiful Decay
This cacophony of giblets, pigs' trotters, external colons and rectums, gummy eyes for nipples and imploded crepe-paper-like epidermises create a space of confusion for the viewer. The work draws one in, yet also repulses at the same time, with its mixture of the animal and the synthesised – its subjects striking poses of beautiful decay.

Van Minnen was born in Providence, Rhode Island, in 1980, and went to art school at Regis University, Denver, Colorado, graduating in 2002. He has exhibited throughout the US and internationally. 'My first influences as a young person were nature field guides, comic books, then artist and sculptor HR Giger, followed by the Surrealists and then various schools of the Old Masters. An interest in contemporary art came much later in life for me.'[2] After graduation, developing a life as an artist was not plain sailing and a host of manual and menial jobs were needed to survive – indeed, at one point a radical change of course was momentarily entertained: 'It was mostly painting nights and weekends for years while working in a variety of warehousing, landscaping or driving jobs. I showed my work a few times between 2003 and 2006 at co-op galleries, but

Christian Rex van Minnen,
Untitled,
2022

below: The work rejoices in creating equivalencies particularly in relation to the human body – a Surrealist tactic. Here the bodies of a deformed human, chicken legs and a Damien Hirst-type jewel-encrusted skull are combined to arresting effect along with, of course, the ubiquitous gummies.

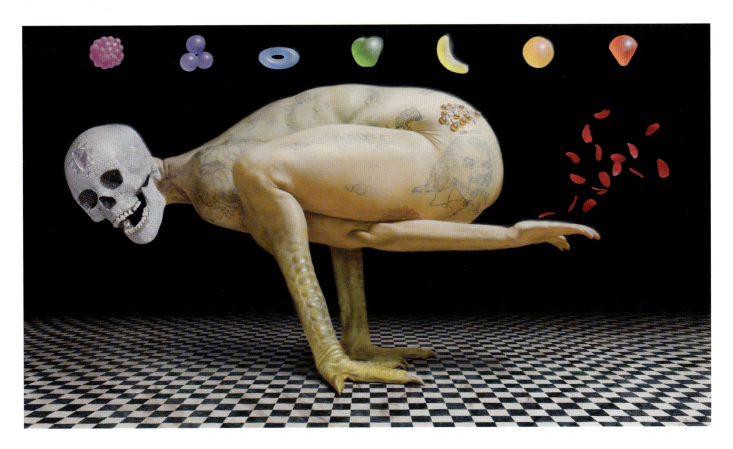

I gave up the idea of working as an artist and went back to get a master's in nonprofit management.'

Having decided that management was not his forte, he reverted to life in the labour market and returned to night-time and evening painting. One day he was injured on a landscaping job and whilst he was recovering he could paint full-time for a few weeks – a moment of epiphany: 'This was in the mid-2000s when I really dug in and tried to learn all this Old Masters stuff. It was also right about the time when social media took off, and I got into the Pop Surrealist movement and was invited to do shows all over the world. That really changed a lot for me, knowing there was this global, alternative art world. It's all mixed up now, but I think that moment in the mid-2000s for figurative artists, globally, was really unique.'

When asked about his historic studio setups, his methodology and whether there is any reliance on the digital world in the production of the work, he replies, 'I've never shared a studio, but I've definitely worked in some odd spaces to save money. My process varies quite a bit, from one extreme of referenceless Surrealism to on occasion using photographs for specific elements. I get frustrated easily with computers and digital processes so that has been hard to incorporate easily.'

Today his studio is a laboratory that investigates the 'mystery of paint' and is the venue for his own artistic self-discovery and what it means to be human or even posthuman. He is also extremely productive. 'These paintings present evidence of a human being earnestly at work with the mystery of paint, this medium that has served us since the dawn of time, trying to get at some sort of deeper truth about who I am, who we are. I work on many paintings at once, all mixed up to allow adequate dry time, so it is hard to say how long they take, end to end.'

Gummy Mannerism for a New Century

It is the heady mix of surrealism and the mundane that gives Van Minnen's work its powerful presence and visceral aesthetic hit – something also inspired by more traditional and older artists he admires. 'One group I keep coming back to is the Schildersbent, or Bentvueghels. They were a group of Dutch painters who travelled to Rome in the 17th century to learn from the Italians, and kind of created a Bacchanalian cult of painting. Some of my favourite paintings came out of that, like Otto Marseus van Schrieck and Willem van Aeslt.' Their portraiture and still lifes have taught Van Minnen their tried and tested protocols of artistic composition, which he continues to use today: 'They are conventions that work very well without a lot of effort. It comes down to a few geometric relationships and the thing "works", that's interesting to me.' For all his studying of the Old Masters, Van Minnen's works are profoundly modern and contemporary.

Much of the work features perhaps the most mundane yet surreal confectionery of all: gummy candies. Their forms, colours and smooth jellied textures inhabit almost everything he produces nowadays, a counterpoint to the darker emphasis of some of his earlier preoccupations and providing light relief. Yet Van Minnen sees the gummy and the dark forms as interchangeable: 'It is a confluence of two streams; experimentation in combining Northern and Italian Renaissance techniques by combining white and toned grounds, and also a solution to having an opposite, or contrasting point, to the melancholic, tenebristic weighty human forms. Having something light and luminous, gravity defying, whimsical and transparent was important to me. It made possible a strange shift in the paintings, where the gummies now take on the role of the repulsive, and the body is more sympathetic, maybe.'

Christian Rex van Minnen,
Untitled,
2023

above: The frogspawn pustules or rancid caviar in this still life might be mistaken for small grapes at first look, but further examination reveals that they have an uncanniness about them, as do the tattooed balls of flesh and gristle.

Christian Rex van Minnen,
Untitled,
2022

left: This cross between the imagined and the real still life incorporates gravity-defying gummies and a hyper-real snake in a glass vessel, and is seared through by a multicolour migraine zigzag.

Christian Rex van Minnen,
Untitled,
2022

left: A gristly, fleshly yet almost abstract still life that feels as though it has been inspired by the butcher's chopping block. It has an intestinal aesthetic, so many of its elements are unrecognisable yet strangely visceral.

Christian Rex van Minnen,
Untitled,
2022

opposite: Eyeless heads and deformed inscribed torsos are a Van Minnen trademark, often with rainbow-like colouring over the eye sockets, nose and mouth – that most important area in normal human communication and conversation.

Frogspawn Pustules

Whilst Van Minnen's output has its own originality and take, the Surrealist tradition, if one may call it that, embodies such traits, fetishes and tropes and has a long history. The distortion of the body caught in posed attitudes of distress and grief or even personal nonchalance about what is happening around it or to it, frequently appears in times of war and societal upheaval. Such tropes are often emblematic and have caused some of art's great perturbations. Two historical examples will suffice. Pablo Picasso's *Guernica* (1937) was inspired by the events of the Spanish Civil War – a nation tearing itself apart, appositely depicted in paint. Likewise, in England, at the zenith of the Second World War and later during its denouement, painter Francis Bacon was exploring the loneliness of the human condition, its movement, visceral vulnerability and metamorphosis in relation to our fears and loathings. Around 1944 he painted what he considered to be his first 'opus', *Three Studies for Figures at the Base of a Crucifixion*. The three figures were the genesis of his artistic endeavours for the rest of his life – almost fifty years. The work consists of a triptych of half-human forms: Furies – hunched, pained, angry mutants mocking and celebrating the crucifixion that is happening, invisibly, above them. However, the fact that it is invisible does not make it any the less disturbing or real. The figure to the left is perched on a plinth, the central figure on a convoluted tripod, and the right-hand figure on a small mat, maybe of grass.

Like Van Minnen's oeuvre they can be read as the demented, smeared products of some grotesque medical/biological experiment, strange barometers of humanity's cruelness to its fellows, morphing and screaming as our exponential technological growth and ethical decay continue. Van Minnen's figures are 'uncanny' as we recognise ourselves within them. We are fearful of the implied violence done to them, yet we empathise with their brooding presence and imagined pain.

Painterly speculations on matters of posthuman epidemiology and dermatology, out-of-control genetics, rampant mitosis, self-harm and pyrotechnics are some of Van Minnen's stock-in-trade. Frogspawn-like pustules also erupt at times, yet the work is stunningly executed, weirdly beautiful and can stop you in your tracks. It provokes thoughts of the body in space and the fact that it is a canvas in its own right, becoming more penetrable and deformable as our technologies, which crossed the Rubicon of our skin long ago, continue to exponentially develop. 'Generally, I like maximalism. I attempt to see harmony in the vibrant contrasts of every type – form, emotion, colour, value, texture. That desire to see this is the driving force, all the motifs and language are in service of that I think.'

Van Minnen's work is unique, rejoicing in old-school painting techniques yet with a super-Surrealist verve addressing the aesthetic conundrums of our time, and a super-saturated colour palette and tribal eviscerations of tagging and marking the flesh. Within his work is the biography and biology of the contemporary era, there to be read in all its flaws and imperfections. ⌂

Notes
1. Xavière Gauthier, *Surréalisme et sexualité*, Paris, 1971, p 211, quoted in Arie Graafland, *Architectural Bodies*, ed Michael Speaks, 010 Publishers (Rotterdam), 1996, p 53.
2. All quotes from an interview with the author, 19 April 2023.

Text © 2024 John Wiley & Sons Ltd.
Images © Christian Rex van Minnen

POSTHUMAN ARCHITECTURES: THEORIES, DESIGN, TECHNOLOGIES AND FUTURES

Olga Bannova is a Research Professor at the University of Houston, Texas, where she is also the Sasakawa International Center for Space Architecture (SICSA) and MS in Space Architecture programme director. She studies orbital and surface habitability, design influences and requirements for different gravity conditions, and design for extreme environments on Earth. She is the author of *Space Architecture: Human Habitats beyond the Planet Earth* (DOM Publishers, 2021), which received the Social Sciences Book Award from the International Academy of Astronautics, and co-author, with Sandra Häuplik-Meusburger, of *Space Architecture Education for Engineers and Architects* (Springer, 2016), as well as many book chapters and technical publications.

Roberto Bottazzi is an architect, researcher and educator based in London. He previously studied in Italy and Canada. He is an Associate Professor at the Bartlett School of Architecture, University College London (UCL), where he directs the Master's in Urban Design. He is the author of *Digital Architecture Beyond Computers: Fragments of a Cultural History of Computational Design* (Bloomsbury, 2018) and co-editor of *Walking Cities: London* (Camberwell Press, 2017). His research analyses the impact of digital technologies on architecture and urbanism, and has been presented and exhibited internationally.

Mario Carpo is the Reyner Banham Professor of Architectural History and Theory at the Bartlett School of Architecture, UCL, and Professor of Architectural Theory at the University of Applied Arts Vienna. His research and publications focus on the relationship among architectural theory, cultural history, and the history of media and design technologies. His book *Architecture in the Age of Printing* (MIT Press, 2001) has been translated into several languages. His most recent books are *Beyond Digital: Design and Automation at the End of Modernity* (2023), *The Second Digital Turn: Design Beyond Intelligence* (2017) and *The Alphabet and the Algorithm* (2011), all published by MIT Press.

Mollie Claypool is co-founder and CEO of Automated Architecture (AUAR) Ltd, and Associate Professor in Architecture at the Bartlett School of Architecture, UCL, where she is Co-Director of AUAR Labs, History & Theory Coordinator in MArch Architectural Design, and Managing Editor of *Prospectives*, an open-access peer-reviewed journal. She is co-author of *Robotic Building: Architecture in the Age of Automation* (Detail, 2019) and the SPACE10 report 'The Digital in Architecture: Then, Now and in the Future' (2019).

Xavier De Kestelier is an architect and Head of Design at Hassell in London, where he leads design technology across all disciplines and regions. Previously he was the co-head of Foster + Partners' internal research and development team, the Specialist Modelling Group. For the last decade, he has been an industry leader in the field of parametric design, digital fabrication and additive manufacturing as well as building up a portfolio of space-related architecture for clients such as NASA, the European Space Agency (ESA), Virgin Galactic and Sierra Space. He is also a Director of Smartgeometry, a non-profit educational organisation for computational design and digital fabrication. He has taught at Syracuse University, the University of Ghent and the Bartlett School of Architecture, UCL.

Paul Dobraszczyk is a lecturer at the Bartlett School of Architecture, UCL. He is the author of many books, the most recent being *Botanical Architecture: Design and the Vegetal* (Reaktion, 2024), *Animal Architecture: Beasts, Buildings and Us* (Reaktion, 2023), and *Architecture and Anarchism: Building Without Authority* (Paul Holberton, 2021). He built the photographic website www.stonesofmanchester.com in 2018 and blogs at www.ragpickinghistory.co.uk.

Alberto Fernández González is an architect, educator and researcher at the University of Chile, and at the Bartlett School of Architecture, UCL, where he is a lecturer and PhD candidate. In 2020 he became an advisory board member of the school's *Prospectives* journal. He was winner of the UIA Celeb Cities 3 at the 2006 Venice Architecture Biennale, of the Archiprix International in 2007, and Holcim Award Next Generation 2008, and was recognised by the Chilean Association of Architects as Best Young Architect of 2009. He is a SIGraDi board member, a co-founder of DigitalFUTURES (Spanish) and a co-founder of Rational Energy Architects, exploring the intersection of AI, solar energy, participatory design and self-generated spaces.

Ariane Lourie Harrison is a principal and co-founder of Harrison Atelier (HAT) and a registered architect in New York State. She is the Coordinator of the Master of Science in Urban Design at the Graduate School of Architecture, Pratt Institute in New York, a lecturer at the Yale School of Architecture in New Haven, Connecticut, where she has taught since 2006, and at the Weitzman School of Design at the University of Pennsylvania in Philadelphia. HAT's work on multi-species design has been internationally recognised, with the Hempcrete Habitats project winning the 2022 Global Architecture and Design Award, and Pollinators Pavilion the AIANY Design Awards 2021.

Sandra Häuplik-Meusburger is a pioneering researcher and architect specialising in socio-spatial sustainable design for terrestrial and extra-terrestrial realms. Based at TU Wien in Vienna, she instructs and guides design studios throughout Europe, the US, UAE and China. She serves as the Academic Director for the Executive MBA in Space Architecture at TU Wien, and the Science Academy's Space course in Lower Austria. An author of multiple acclaimed books on space architecture and extreme environment habitability, she is a member of the International Academy of Astronautics (IAA) and chairs the Space Architecture Technical Committee at the American Institute of Aeronautics and Astronautics (AIAA).

Tyson Hosmer is an architect, researcher and educator working at the intersection of design, computation, AI and robotics. He is Founder and CEO of Autonomy Lab Ltd. He is a Senior Lecturer and the Director of the Architectural Design (AD) Master's programme at the Bartlett School of Architecture, UCL, where he directs the Living Architecture Lab (RC3). He is also a Senior Associate Researcher and head of the ZHA-Social research group with Zaha Hadid Architects. His research focuses on autonomous reconfigurable architectural systems with artificial intelligence, cognitive agent-based systems, and generative design models with deep learning.

Steven Hutt is a practising RIBA Chartered Architect, wildlife researcher and proponent of speculative ecological posthuman design. The winner of the twelfth internationally acclaimed RIBA Norman Foster Travelling Scholarship, and author of *East of Eden: New Urban Ecologies in the Far East,* he has worked at Foster + Partners on a number of high-profile international projects across Europe, the Middle East, North America and Oceania. His ongoing urban wildlife research can be found at www.wildercities.com.

CONTRIBUTORS

Jonathan Irawan is Computational Design Lead at Hassell. Having previously worked on multidisciplinary projects across the globe, he incorporates a wider perspective in the formulation of design solutions. He bridges the gap in design technology research between academia and industry implementation by constant experimentation. At the centre of his explorations is the relationship and interactivity between architecture and their respective social agencies. His body of work focuses on the implementation of experimental and innovative design and construction methodologies, highly responsive adaptive systems, behavioural analysis and simulation.

Sylvia Lavin is a Professor of History and Theory of Architecture at Princeton University, New Jersey. Her work explores the limits of architecture across a wide spectrum of historical periods. Her publications include *Quatremère de Quincy and the Invention of a Modern Language of Architecture* (MIT Press, 1992), *Form Follows Libido: Architecture and Richard Neutra in a Psychoanalytic Culture* (MIT Press, 2005) and *Everything Loose Will Land: 1970s Art and Architecture in Los Angeles* (Verlag für moderne Kunst Nürnberg, 2013). She received her PhD from Columbia University in New York, and was formerly Professor and Chair in the Department of Architecture and Urban Design at the University of California, Los Angeles (UCLA). She is currently working on a new book, *Building Sylvan Media*.

Jacopo Leveratto is a Senior Lecturer at the Department of Architecture and Urban Studies at the Politecnico di Milano, Milan, where he focuses his research on radical forms of habitability and posthuman architecture. Local Principal Investigator of the European Research *en/counter/points* (2018–22) and head of Walden Architects during the 2021 Seoul Biennale on Architecture and Urbanism, he is now a coordinating member of the Italian National Biodiversity Future Center. Besides having authored numerous publications in peer-reviewed journals and edited volumes, he published a monographic work on the theme titled *Posthuman Architectures: A Catalogue of Archetypes* (ORO Editions, 2021).

Levent Ozruh is an architectural designer and space architect at Hassell, contributing to the research-based design proposals for the European Space Agency (ESA). He also worked on future commercial space stations for Sierra Space. Outside Hassell, he runs OZRUH, a London-based architectural design studio that explores the intersection of advanced manufacturing, procedural systems and bottom-up design thinking. He has taught design studios at the Bartlett School of Architecture, UCL, and at the Institute for Advanced Architecture of Catalonia (IAAC). Most recently, he co-founded the AAVS Moonshot, a school focusing on architectural design in the second space age. Prior to finishing his diploma studies at the Bartlett, he worked as a researcher at the Massachusetts Institute of Technology (MIT).

Colbey Reid is Professor and Chair of Fashion Studies at Columbia College Chicago. She co-edited and contributed to *Design, Mediation, and the Posthuman* (Lexington Books, 2016) and has published articles on the intellectual history of glamour, the religiosity of American cocktail culture, design flaws, Victorian cybernetics, statistical aesthetics, brand secret micro-collectives, the technicity of fashion and interior design, and the haptics of reading. She is co-author, with Dennis Weiss, of the monograph *Designing the Domestic Posthuman* (Bloomsbury, 2023).

Brent Sherwood is a space architect. Until recently he was Senior Vice President, Space Systems Development for Blue Origin. He previously led the Jet Propulsion Laboratory's Innovation Foundry and Solar System Mission Formulation, and also led Boeing teams for human space system concepts, Space Station module manufacturing, and business development for entrepreneurial civil and commercial space initiatives. He has published extensively about the exploration, development and settlement of Space. He is an Associate Fellow of the American Institute of Aeronautics and Astronautics, corresponding member of the International Academy of Astronautics (AIAA), and the 2021 recipient of the American Society of Civil Engineers Columbia Medal.

Neil Spiller is Editor of 𝐷, and was previously Hawksmoor Chair of Architecture and Landscape and Deputy Pro Vice Chancellor at the University of Greenwich in London. Prior to this he was Vice Dean at the Bartlett School of Architecture, UCL. He has made an international reputation as an architect, designer, artist, teacher, writer and polemicist. He is the founding director of the Advanced Virtual and Technological Architecture Research (AVATAR) group, which continues to push the boundaries of architectural design and discourse in the face of the impact of 21st-century technologies. Its current preoccupations include augmented and mixed realities and other metamorphic technologies.

Dennis Weiss is a Professor of Philosophy at York College of Pennsylvania, specialising in contemporary trends in the philosophy of technology and media, posthumanism and cultural studies. He is the editor of *Interpreting Man* (Davies Group Publishers, 2003) and co-editor of and contributor to *Design, Mediation, and the Posthuman* (Lexington Books, 2016). He has also published essays exploring the intersection of philosophy, technology and science fiction. He is co-author, with Colbey Reid, of the monograph *Designing the Domestic Posthuman* (Bloomsbury, 2023).

Andrew Witt is a designer who works at the intersection of architecture, digital media and culture. He is an Associate Professor in Practice of Architecture at Harvard University and co-founder, with Tobias Nolte, of Certain Measures, a design studio that applies imagination and data to trans-scalar spatial design problems. Their work is in the permanent collection of the Centre Pompidou, Paris, and has been exhibited at the Barbican Centre, London, and the Museum of the Future, Dubai, among others. He is the author of *Formulations: Architecture, Mathematics, and Culture* (MIT Press, 2022), a history of mathematics in modern architecture.

What is *Architectural Design*?

Founded in 1930, *Architectural Design* (△) is an influential and prestigious publication. It combines the currency and topicality of a newsstand journal with the rigour and production qualities of a book. With an almost unrivalled reputation worldwide, it is consistently at the forefront of cultural thought and design.

Issues of △ are edited either by the journal Editor, Neil Spiller, or by an invited Guest-Editor. Renowned for being at the leading edge of design and new technologies, △ also covers themes as diverse as architectural history, the environment, interior design, landscape architecture and urban design.

Provocative and pioneering, △ inspires theoretical, creative and technological advances. It questions the outcome of technical innovations as well as the far-reaching social, cultural and environmental challenges that present themselves today.

For further information on △ and purchasing single issues see:

https://onlinelibrary.wiley.com/journal/15542769

Individual backlist issues of △ are available as books for purchase starting at £29.99 / US$45.00

wiley.com

Americas
E: cs-journals@wiley.com
T: +1 877 762 2974

Europe, Middle East and Africa
E: cs-journals@wiley.com
T: +44 (0)18 6577 8315

Asia Pacific
E: cs-journals@wiley.com
T: +65 6511 8000

Japan (for Japanese-speaking support)
E: cs-japan@wiley.com
T: +65 6511 8010

Visit our Online Customer Help
available in 7 languages at
www.wileycustomerhelp.com/ask

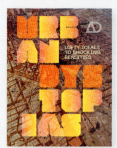

Volume 93 No 1
ISBN 978-1-119-83399-4

Volume 93 No 2
ISBN 978-1-119-83835-7

Volume 93 No 3
ISBN 978-1-119-83442-7

Volume 93 No 4
ISBN 978-1-119-98396-5

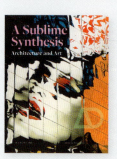

Volume 93 No 5
ISBN 978-1-394-17079-1

Volume 93 No 6
ISBN 978-1-394-16354-0